COMPLIMENTARY COPY
Submitted for review purposes
by Ivy House Publishing Group

NOT FOR RESALE

AMERICA'S
BACKDOOR

America's Backdoor

Vernon Alfred Holmes

Ivy House
Publishing Group

www.ivyhousebooks.com

PUBLISHED BY IVY HOUSE PUBLISHING GROUP
5122 Bur Oak Circle, Raleigh, NC 27612
United States of America
919-782-0281
www.ivyhousebooks.com

ISBN: 1-57197-352-4
Library of Congress Control Number: 2002113583

Copyright © 2003 Vernon Alfred Holmes
All rights reserved, which includes the right to
reproduce this book or portions thereof in any form whatsoever
except as provided by the U.S. Copyright Law.

Printed in the United States of America

ACKNOWLEDGMENTS

This book is dedicated to my grandfather, Erick Alfred Holm, who had a deeply committed survival mentality and a love of hard labor. In describing my grandfather, I'd say he was an individual possessing a firmness and perseverance of purpose. Nothing could divert him from his chosen direction. He was a powerful character. In his youth, he became habituated to the hunting life and the observation of animals. He was a scrupulous man. Whatever he undertook in life was as if selected and implanted by nature.

Given his character, I can think of nothing more fun than researching his life and putting it down on paper. And, I have had the luck of having my grandfather's stories narrated to me by my father, Raymond Lester Holmes.

I would like to thank my wife, Diane Jean Holmes, for her divine generosity in not condemning what I felt so many had a right to know. Her energy, enthusiasm, and humor made my work possible. I would also like to thank my dear Aunt Gladys Muller for putting down her deck of cards long enough to dig out birth and death dates from cemetery locations that only she would know. I also thank my dear cousins, Reverend William and Diana Welk, for having documents translated from Swedish to English, and the fortitude for pushing me to complete this work. Thanks also go to my dear uncle, Robert Lace, Sr., for his valuable time and wonderful facts, and my dear uncle, Donald Holmes, Sr., for his life experiences that he related to me.

Erick Alfred Holm
1878-1925

PREFACE

We first meet seven-year-old Erick Holm alone in the frightening Lotorp forest of southern Sweden. The year was December 1885. Erick, the narrator of this gripping true-life saga, was sent out by his father, Johan, to hunt and trap in order to provide food for the entire family and to try to head off impending starvation. Erick contended with the harsh winter elements and predators of the woods. Soon after, the family made a forced journey across Sweden, trying to escape decades of famine, and seeking a brighter future in the new world of America. They went on to experience a harrowing voyage across the North Atlantic on a cursed immigration vessel known as the "Coffin Ship." The ship was, in actuality, a semi man-of-war that took a surprising entry route into the North American continent down Canada's St. Lawrence River. The vessel continued into the Great Lakes until it reached Chicago, Illinois, the final debarkation point.

In telling the story of my Swedish heritage, this book paints a striking portrait of hardy and courageous pioneer spirits who endured hardship and deprivation in order to start a new life in an often hostile, alien land.

As I share this important chapter of the American immigrant experience, I articulate my buoyant pride for this most unforgettable family who met every challenge thrown at them with pragmatic good humor and uncompromisingly stalwart ethics.

This is a story of my grandparents, all of whom were Swedish men and women. They possessed stout hearts, willing hands, and robust health, and knew at least the rudiments of some useful trade. My grandmothers and great-grandmothers—God bless them!—were worthy consorts of their men who laid low the giants of the forests and made the wilderness blossom with fields of wheat, corn, and potatoes. They knew nothing of whining or feeling tired. They didn't have soft, velvety hands, but they did have gentle, tender, mothering hearts. They could not paint on canvas or play the piano, but they could spin, knit, and weave. These dear souls could drive a nail as well as their younger daughters and could handle a yoke of oxen. They were expert at using the pitchfork and rake as well as the broom and mop.

My grandmother did not prepare fancy foods such as chicken salad and lemon meringue pie, but prepared wholesome flatbrod, mylsa, brim, and Swedish limpa, the kinds of foods on which a hundred generations of Swedish foresters, farmers, and seamen had been raised. A flatbrod was made with yeast and had a smooth appearance and a tasteless crust. It was baked in a 13- or 14-inch tin with a hole in the middle. After removal from the hearth, a corn broom handle was run through the bread's center hole and this was placed outside for cooling. Brinn was a flat level, hard tack which, when scorched or singed for appearance, looked like a darkened graham cracker. Sailors would take large quantities on their voyages. Swedish limpa rye bread was a daily staple made from rye meal and served for breakfast, lunch, and supper. All meals were served with mjocka, an unpasteurized cow milk. A "pig in a poke" was a runt pig in a burlap sack before being cooked and served at meal time.

An overall Swedish favorite was lutfisk, "lut" meaning lye. This was a North Sea cod, dried for six or seven weeks, then submerged in a crock combined with water, lye, and salt for another week. This was boiled, covered with a cream sauce, and served for supper. A person either loved it or hated it, as the smell and appearance were atrocious to many. The odor from this dish often took days to leave a cabin.

My Swedish ancestors were ignorant of the English language, laws, and institutions of their adopted country. Indeed, in this respect, they were heavily handicapped. They had not a single newspaper and not a soul with whom they could communicate outside their Swedish community. But even though my Swedish immigrant ancestors were ignorant of English, they were not illiterate. They had books and could read them. By and by, astonished Americans were forced to confess that, "Them there Swedes are almost as white as we are and they can read too." Books were few in most Swedish homes. Only the Bible and some of Luther's writings could be found.

The houses of my ancestors in the Swedish community of Chicago were made up of log cabins, tarpaper shanties, and dugouts. Men and women alike dressed in blue drill or in coarse homespun brought with them from the old country. They carried everything in their brightly painted chests. The Holm women did not wear hats as we would know them today, but instead wore old country kerchiefs. Carpets, kerosene lamps, coal stoves, sewing machines, reapers, threshing machines, top buggies, stoughton wagons, half pants, and button shoes were things not even dreamed of as yet. The Stoughton wagon was a heavy industrial wagon used to haul armament, like cast cannons and gunpowder. Its counterpart, the Conestoga, had a white canvas roof. Both wagons were called "the camels of the prairies," or "wagon trains." Men all wore suspenders to keep their britches from falling to the floor.

From among these Swedish pioneers also came the pioneers of the Swedish Lutheran Church. It is safe to say that America never saw, and never will see, a more hardy, plucky and successful pioneer spirit than that found among the sons and daughters of old Sweden. My Swedish ancestors were poor, but not paupers. They did not come to America to panhandle, steal, or sponge off their neighbors. It was not their ambition to be organ grinders, peanut venders, or rag pickers. They came to make an honest living by the sweat of their brows. The rough frontier town of Chicago did not intimidate them. In the face of savages, prowling beasts, blizzards, winds that never stopped, and hardships of every description, this army of brave and sturdy Swedish families advanced civilization to what we know it today.

CHAPTER ONE

Erick added more kindling onto his now smoldering fire, trying desperately to warm his numb, half-frozen fingers. His chattering teeth were the only sounds to be heard except for a distant wolf cry. As usual, Erick set up his base camp deep in the frozen tundra of the Lotorp forest. This time of year, southern Sweden was, after all, a dangerous place for anyone to be alone. Chilled to the bone and shivering, he had the knowledge and experience to do what had to be done. He looked much older than seven.

Erick was no stranger to these woods. Being alone in them was nothing new for this young hunter and trapper. He knew of the constant dangers that lurked just moments away. Erick's father, Johan, had taught Erick well, but his father was not with him on this trapping trip. Johan Holm was laid out at home, battling back from a life-threatening hunting accident. He had been relegated to the family's feather bed. The past six weeks of bed rest was driving Erick's father crazy. With no fresh meat on the table and the pantry empty, Erick had to step up as the oldest child. The full weight of providing food for the family had fallen squarely on Erick's not-so-broad shoulders.

The year was 1885 and Erick was out of school. Erick's one room schoolhouse was closed every December due to the long and harsh Swedish winters and also the Christmas holidays. This time of year, the woods would be full of game of all sorts.

So it was that Erick found himself alone in the wilderness facing the biggest challenge of his young life. There was another howl from a wolf, only this time it was quite a bit closer. Again and again the howling pierced the quiet of the woods. Sparks flew higher as Erick poked and prodded the now blazing flames of his fire. Another howl from the woods broke the silence. He reached over to slip his rifle from its buckskin sheath.

Moving his head from side to side, he peered desperately into the blackness of the night. "Nothing," he thought out loud, trying hard to visualize any silhouette against the backdrop of blackness. He looked intently for a set of yellow eyes staring back at him. No matter how hard he looked, he couldn't see the predators. He was a smart and talented boy and he knew the wolves would wait patiently for any small mistake that he might make. He decided that since his unwanted company was so close, he wouldn't lay down in front of the blazing fire. Tonight he would sit up through the night. Each time the fire would grow low, Erick would add more firewood. He tried to keep a crackling blaze, if only to reassure himself that he would remain safe throughout the night.

Oh, he thought to himself, *this will be a great trapping day.* With dawn only a few hours away, Erick sat with his back against a big old oak tree and covered himself with the wool blankets his mother had carefully packed onto one of his two sleds. He looked up to the heavens toward the Big and Little Dippers. The sky held a thousand stars, all twinkling and looking down on the young trapper. They seemed to say, "Tomorrow will be a better day."

Erick felt totally alone. He had trapped alone before, but always much closer to home. This was new, being more than a day away from home. His father wasn't there sitting alongside him by the fire to advise and guide him. Nor was he there to help with his decision-making. Erick was completely alone except for his distant companions, the wolves.

His wool blankets kept him from shivering and shaking. For the first time all night, Erick felt warm. He tried closing his eyes, but sleep wouldn't come. Each time his eyes would grow heavy and close, the howling from the black forest's edge would awaken him.

He sat staring into the flames thinking of stories his father had told him about the Lotorp woods, the woods he now found himself deep within. Father had told all his mysterious and frightening adventure stories sitting at home in front of a roaring fire. Somehow they took on a whole different perspective here alone in the immense, forbidding woods. Erick tried to block out his father's tales from his mind but he couldn't. This being his first night out alone, Erick knew that he shouldn't let his imagination run away, uncontrolled and untethered. Hard as he tried, he couldn't block from his mind the frightening and detailed images of the stories. Time alone in these woods only made his subconscious mind and imagination work overtime.

Erick knew that the wolves didn't necessarily hunt down men or, for that matter, seven-year-old boys. The wolves most likely had been trailing an old or injured elk when they came across his smoke and fire. These were the wolves' woods, even more so than young Erick's. After all, the wolves had been here for thousands of years.

It would not be unusual for his father to come home after a hunting trip with a twelve- or fourteen-point buck to feed the family. With nothing but time and his strong imagination, Erick thought he too would come across a giant buck to take home, not only to feed the family but also to make his father proud of him. The woods were full of game, both big and small. He was not primarily on a venison hunt, but was here for setting traps. This trip was for beaver, mink, and fox. Erick had a full sled-load of animal traps that had to be set in the next few days. His father had taught him that trapping was a very dangerous method of gathering food, but a necessary evil required for fur trading. The family needed furs to trade for grain, flour, and corn.

Erick remembered the frightening tales these woods had inspired. It was not a normal place for a seven-year-old to be alone. Villagers told haunting stories of evil spirits that abounded in the Lotorp woods and waters. Some said footprints had been found deep in the woods that were not human or animal. Tales were told of some beasts that lived in these woods. Older villagers called them the Namekagan men of Lotorp. The legend had been passed on from generation to generation throughout the ages, whispered about at community gatherings and long after church had let out. Did these wild beasts or prehistoric men actually exist or were these tales dreamed up under the influence of whiskey and rum? With these thoughts, a chill ran through Erick from head to toe. He had to stop these wild thoughts or sleep would never come.

Erick added more wood to the fire, not only to stay warm but also to add more light to his darkened encampment. His mind shot back to the idea that this beast could very well be out in the blackness beyond his camp. Erick couldn't shake the thoughts of a Namekagan man that could be hiding behind every tree in the dark shadows on this cold winter night.

The story first surfaced many years before Erick's father was a boy. Like all stories, it seemed to escalate around the campfires of trappers where each generation of storyteller would add onto the original tale. Erick remembered his father's version of the tale. During one of the harshest, coldest winters in Sweden's known history, a family of potato farmers was trying to relocate from the northern province down to the middle of the country, known as the breadbasket of Sweden. As the story went, it was so cold that branches of white birch snapped off and were piled along the forest bed like cordwood so as to make traveling through the forest next to impossible. The farmers' mustaches and beards were frozen solid from moisture given off as they trekked through the forest of broken limbs and boughs.

The farming family was made up of a husband and wife, two small daughters, three older sons, and a grandfather and grandmother. The temperature was thirty below. To make matters worse, the snow had not yet crusted over, so with each step the family would be waist deep in snow. The farmers now knew they were on a death march as they set their traps. Their eyes were almost frozen shut from the bitter cold when out of the forest came the Namekagan men. These were trappers and hunters of the past who had gone mad from the cold, hunger, and starvation. They came from the dark shadows and savagely beat and butchered the family. Their body parts were put into neat little stacks like cordwood. They ate those farmers and fed their bones to the dogs. Since the dogs had eaten their bones, no evidence of this savagery and cannibalism was ever found. However, the spirits of the farmers still haunted those woods that young Erick had claimed to be his. Erick believed that some of the spirits were angry and that they haunted the woods still in hopes of seeking revenge for their despicable and horrible deaths.

Erick slept through the night with an eerie and unsettling calm. He was apprehensive of the day ahead of him.

Erick awoke shivering beneath his mother's woolen blankets. Opening his eyes, he glanced around his camp. He was not surprised to find his fire had gone out and that only a few embers still had a slight glow. A small wisp of smoke rose from the fire pit. Glancing toward the eastern ridge of the Lotorp forest, he saw the first rays of light filter through the birch and poplar trees. Knowing a long, hard day of trapping lay before him, he began cutting kindling and stoking his fire to regain the flames that had died out. Erick figured his fire had gone out hours earlier, but the flames came up fast and furious, licking tenderly at the freshly cut kindling.

Warmth spread through Erick as he imagined the wonderful day that lay before him. But then a not so pleasant surprise began to fall: snow. The snow started as a light and gentle dusting, but Erick could not chance coming back at nightfall with no place to bed down. He quickly built himself a shelter of white birch. The soft wood of the birch yielded under the cold steel of his ax. As the dawn's early light sifted through the tree line, he finished his task and had what he considered one mighty fine temporary home. He cut off two generously thick slices of elk thigh and started breakfast. He laughed out loud as he remembered something Grandfather Ernst had said about Erick's mother: "The woman can cook."

Out of the early morning darkness, a lone wolf howled a long and mournful song as if looking for its mate. The howling persisted, shattering the quiet and cutting through the icy cold morning air. Erick knew some hunters and trappers had gone mad listening to these tunes when out in the wilderness for months at a time. Some had even been eaten by the same wolves they had been hunting. Erick realized that danger was always present and hung heavy in the forest air.

By now, his fire was high and blazing, perfect for making what Erick called "wilderness toast." His mother's homemade bread was frozen, so he sawed off a piece and pierced it with a birch switch to toast over the fire. The elk didn't take long to brown and the bread turned a toasty cinnamon color. How wonderful breakfast tasted over an open fire in the woods, Erick's woods.

He carefully packed his sled and backpack for his trapping expedition. He had food, clothing, bullets, matches, and extra boots. He then slit down dry kindling. He would use this kindling for his evening fire, once he returned to camp. Erick knew he would be tired and exhausted after a full day of hauling his sled and setting animal traps. After such a hard day, the last thing he would want to do would be to chop kindling.

His sled was full of animal traps, a change of clothing, and a second pair of boots, as well as plenty of matches. "Let's go, let's go," he muttered under his breath. The continuing light snow was beautiful as Erick walked along pulling his sled behind him. It didn't take him long to go through the woods and down a slight embankment to one of his favorite places to be in the summer: Potato Lake. His father had told him the story of how the name Potato Lake originally came from two surveyors who had surveyed the area around the Lotorp lakes. The lake, in fact, was the shape of a potato, but certainly not a round potato. It was the shape of any potato Erick's mother would have thrown into her stew pot.

Erick thought of the summer before when he was younger and more impressionable. He and his whole family had come through the woods to picnic and fish for the ever-present pike. The lake held two types of pike: the pickerel and northern. Both were finger licking good when fried over an open campfire. The deliciousness of the fried pike only came alive under the experienced fingers of Erick's mother and her secret seasoning. It always seemed as if Mother would be busy cleaning pike and frying them up in her skillet as little Charles found a way to get into trouble. Memories of picnicking on Potato Lake always made Erick remember the constant mischief his little brother would get into. Charles was not at all like Erick, but what could you expect? After all, he was only five years old.

Erick allowed himself no more thoughts of home or family. He was here for the purpose of gathering food for the long winter that lay ahead. It was futile to look for animal tracks since it had been snowing for hours. Erick drove in his first steel stake, right at the water's edge. He then chopped a hole in the lake ice so his trap would go in beneath the water. For bait, he placed a frozen piece of intestine on the holder in the trap, opened the trap wide, and set the trigger mechanism. His first trap was set and ready for a beaver.

A wave of excitement flushed over him. *I am Erick the Trapper,* he thought. To him, that sounded great, it sounded right. *Erick the Great,* he thought, *now that sounds even better.* He decided that he had patted himself on the back enough and that it was time to get on with his business of trapping. Up to this point, Erick had been so busy setting his first trap that he hadn't noticed the snow still falling. He wondered if it was an omen of things to come or if it was all part of a scheme set up by the Namekagan to lure young Erick into their own sinister trap. *No time, no time to dwell on such thoughts. A sinister trap. How farfetched,* he told himself. Taking a tighter hold on his sled's rope, he pushed on.

He stopped briefly to look through the continuing snow, visualizing in his mind the location of his first trap. He moved on about a quarter of a mile. He remembered the cove he was in had been where he had fished last summer. He remembered scores of young and old beavers swimming tirelessly through Potato Lake's pristine, clear, spring-fed waters. The beavers had worked effortlessly that summer, cutting down birch and poplar trees. They seemed like miniature lumberjacks. All the trees they cut down fell partially into the water. Beavers were the ultimate engineers and brilliant builders. They could change the course of rivers, streams, and creeks. Their efforts sometimes created ponds and miniature lakes. Oh, how they could cut, haul, build, and create so many good things in nature. All spring, summer, and fall they would work long hours each day, barely taking time out to have families full of little beaver babies. With that thought, Erick put beavers out of his mind and tried to concentrate on trapping. *Trapper Erick the Great won't be killing little babies of any kind, never, ever,* Erick thought to himself.

He pulled a second trap from the sled, along with an intestine his mother had carefully packed to be used as bait for his traps. The intestines were neatly wrapped so they would come apart easily while he set his traps. Thoughts of his mother flashed through his head. He was so lucky to have such a wonderful mother. Mother could do, after all, everything a man could do. She could start a fire, cut down trees, chop firewood, fish, and hunt, in addition to cooking, baking, and knitting. With his stomach growling so loudly, he knew he had to take his mind off of his mother's cooking and baking. He opened the trap after driving the stake into the frozen lake bottom. His second trap was now set. He felt quite proud that things were going according to plan. *Trapping,* he thought, *will feed my family, plus the skins, if dressed out with care, can bring a good return at the general store. Possibly even a piece of hard candy or licorice.* Oh, how Erick's mouth watered for his weakness: licorice.

The weather just wouldn't cooperate. Erick shivered in the icy mist and stinging sleet. He looked back over his shoulder as the distant howls of the wolves seemed to be getting closer and closer. He couldn't let them get the better of him. Erick continued pulling the sled, briefly stopping to tie his hood tighter and pull up his scarf so only his eyes were visible. Erick looked like the Ghost of Christmas Past, snow-covered and with miniature icicles clinging to his clothing. "Why did I ever volunteer to do this?" he asked himself out loud. "After all, I am only seven years old. Well, I'm almost eight, in only a few short months." He was shivering again and wishing he could remain a little boy, if only for a little while longer.

The coldness made him think how great it would be to have a cup of coffee. Why hadn't he stayed in camp a bit longer and made some? His mother would always say, "Erick, coffee will stunt your growth." With that, Mother would always add sugar and ample amounts of their cow's cream. She added so much cream in fact, that it was like drinking coffee straight from the cow. His father would always peer over his glasses at the breakfast table and smile his most loving smile. The slow sipping of his hot coffee would follow this.

Once again, Erick slowed down as a howl came from the woods to his east. He looked down at the side of his sled, if only to reassure himself that his rifle was ready and loaded. Not that he would want to, but there was always the chance that he might have to challenge the wolves.

Erick knew of the lake's springs for his father had shown him all five. He knew precisely where each was located and knew of the dangers of getting too close. The summer before, Father and Grandfather Ernst had brought Erick along on their fishing trip to Potato Lake. Father and Grandfather had carried the small boat through the woods, while Erick helped carry the poles and their shore lunch. As his father and grandfather paddled along, they would stop at each of the five springs. Grandfather would hold Erick tightly and allow him to lean over the boat's side and look down at the lake bottom. If his mother had been along, Father as well as Grandfather would have received a good scolding for allowing Erick to hang over the boat's side.

Grandfather would say, "Look straight down and you will see a hole in the lake."

"Yes, I see the hole in the lake, Grandfather," Erick would reply. Through the crystal clear, pristine water, Erick saw a round black hole in the lake bottom.

"It's a spring," Father said, "and look closely at the fast-moving water coming out of the hole. The spring water comes up through the earth from miles below and has so much force that the ice can never form in the coldest of winters. If anything at all, it only becomes inches thick and can never support the weight of animals or men. The water is so cold coming up out of the earth that fish cannot live anywhere near the springs. These springs are actually the poorest places on the whole lake to fish. You will never find any fish near the springs." And with that explanation, they paddled on.

It seemed to Erick that it had been only yesterday that he was right here at this very spot, fishing from his grandfather's boat. Warm summer memories were a wonderful break from the bitter reality of the cold, snow-filled winter day. He thought of his mother's warm kitchen with heat radiating from the fireplace hearth. He imagined her there now. She was most likely worrying about him and his safety. Erick peered with one hand slightly covering his eyes so as to see through the now-blinding snow. He wished he was back home or, at the very least, at his temporary home under the birch branches out of the cold wind.

He knew Potato Creek was somewhere very close ahead now, so he had to pay attention. He didn't want to go past the creek. He had big plans for setting traps along the Potato. He recalled walking along the ridgeline during the summer above the creek and seeing all the downed birch and poplar trees. Erick knew that the beaver were plentiful back along the whole length of the creek. He remembered not far along the creek, maybe back about a mile, was the first of two beaver dams Erick had witnessed. The dams—these huge walls of sticks, tree branches, logs, and mud—were a miraculous sight. The beavers had dammed up the creek at two points. In between the two dams, these little engineers had created their very own swimming hole.

"What a sight," Erick remembered. "Generations of beaver swimming and playing in their very own swimming pool. It seemed like Father and I watched them for hours. We all temporarily forgot about fishing and just sat down to enjoy the large family of beavers. Father would tease and point his finger toward one of the beavers and say, 'Why look, it's Grandpa Ernst and Grandma Anna hauling branches down the creek.' Father said that if you looked closely at the beaver house, you could see the mother beaver preparing dinner for her children. The children dived into the pool from what could be envisioned as a high diving board." Oh, what a vivid imagination Erick had.

He pushed those thoughts out of his mind and got on with the task of setting traps. Erick finally recognized the mouth leading into Potato Creek. The cold wind whistled through the pines and an eerie feeling crept through him. He bent down and separated some of the traps on the sled. He thought the creek's mouth would be a fine location to set a fox trap. Maybe, if luck would have it, he could trap a coyote or two. What a hero he would be to bring home a coyote. Erick dwelled on thoughts of trapping one of those pesky wolves that had been following him for miles. *What if a wolf actually does stumble into one of my traps, purely by accident of course?* Erick wondered. *Well, I guess I would be known throughout the Lotorp area as the youngest trapper in all of Lotorp.* He liked those thoughts. He liked them really well.

Erick drove his steel stake through the crusted snow as deep as he could. This trap was the largest his father owned. He cut up an intestine from his bait bag, opened the trap carefully, turned the safety lever off, and it was set, ready for a fox, he hoped.

Erick listened intently for anything that might be out of the ordinary, once again allowing his thoughts of the forest shadows to overtake his trapping concentration. Erick pulled up his sled rope and proceeded down the creek's shore. Now he had beaver on his mind. He decided to chop some holes along the stream's edge, so as to lower his baited traps down deep beneath the thickness of ice. Erick looked over to where he had driven in the fox trap, measured off the distance in his mind, and proceeded to chop his first hole into Potato Creek. Here at the mouth of the creek, he thought, would be a most ideal location for placement of three beaver traps. Erick finished chopping his holes, baited the three traps, and carefully lowered them down into the cold, clear water. He noticed the current flowing beneath his chopped holes and remembered his father's instructions and warnings about Potato Creek. Father had said, "Stay off of the creek unless you are positive about the safety of the ice."

The snow continued to fall and Erick briefly looked up the creek embankment on his side of the creek. He caught a glimpse of some movement darting between the pines. Maybe it was the Namekagan men. He reached for his rifle only to remember it was on his sled on the other side of the creek. Ripples of sweat ran down his forehead. *This is just like me to be caught unarmed and unprepared for my last stand,* thought Erick.

He knelt down low to the snow and focused on the embankment again. This time he caught sight of what was really moving slowly from pine to pine and it was not the Namekagan men. It was a cougar. Noting her length, Erick figured she must be full-grown. She was long and sleek, tan in color, with an enormously long bowed tail. Erick shuddered as a cold chill passed through him. He knew for sure that it was a cougar and that meant extreme danger.

Erick saw his sled across the creek with his rifle leaning gently up against it. He continued to watch the embankment but saw nothing now. That could be good or it could be bad. He had to do something, so he started walking across the creek toward his rifle. When he reached it, he swung it up to his shoulder in a defensive movement. Erick scanned the embankment for what seemed like forever. He saw no more cougar movement and heard no sounds from the forest except for the constantly falling snow. He decided to get back to trapping. His mind focused on the real possibility of the cougar following his every movement from some hidden vantage point, high up in a tree.

Erick chopped another hole in the ice and proceeded to set another beaver trap. Finishing with this trap, he stood up and took a moment to look around at the winter wonderland surrounding him. The sleet and snow had frozen on the soft poplar and birch trees. The pines were heavily laden with ice and snow, so much in fact that their branches hung down straight toward the snow base. Now he couldn't see into the forest at all. Erick shook from the realization that he was very lucky to be alive. He determined to never again be separated from his rifle out in the wilderness. Leaving his rifle on the opposite side of the creek may have been the dumbest thing he had ever done. He decided no one in the family really needed to know anything about the incident. Especially about the cougar lurking somewhere close by, waiting for Erick to blunder one last time.

Erick remembered the time his father sat him down to tell him all the dangers of crossing a creek on ice. But he had chopped holes in this ice and knew it was four inches thick. Just then, there was a sudden flash of tan racing across the creek toward Erick. His mind darted from cougar to rifle in a tenth of a second.

CHAPTER TWO

With no warning, Erick's right leg disappeared beneath him and went into the frozen water of the creek. He realized that the ice had held and only his right leg was in the creek. His left hand reached the rifle stock and he pulled the rifle to him. His finger found the trigger and he fired toward the racing cougar. He missed, but at the loud sound of the rifle, the cougar turned direction and ran straight up the embankment. Erick's mind quickly forgot about the cougar, if only briefly, and focused on his survival.

Erick's thoughts were now on his leg, which was completely below the ice. He glanced around and found himself exactly midstream. It was the same distance to each side of the shore. His leg was cold from the water, but he felt he had to reload the rifle for fear of the cougar realizing his vulnerability. After all, Erick was stuck in the ice and could be made a tasty dinner at any moment. He quickly reloaded and laid his rifle down a couple of feet away, yet readily available to grab if he needed to.

First things first. He had to pull his right leg out of the ice-cold water. He slowly pulled up on his leg, but the ice around him began to crack and buckle. The ice dropped about four inches, but held tight from sending him down under the blackness of the moving creek water. His father had told him that streams and creeks always have moving water, especially if they contain natural springs. Erick was in a precarious position, but he knew he had to get his right leg out and get it out quickly. All around him, he saw hundreds of small cracks in the ice. It looked as if he was caught in a spider's web, except the spider was Erick. His heart was beating so loudly he thought his mother could hear it back at the cabin. His heart beat faster and faster as wave after wave of panic swept over his body. His eyes were wide open as if trying to gather every detail of the disaster he found himself alone in. He imagined the ice at last giving its final crack under his weight and pulling him down beneath the black water. He could see the water rushing his thrashing body along underneath the shelf of ice, as he swallowed creek water until he finally drowned.

Erick moved slowly, putting his weight on his rifle that was laid out across the cracks. The ice seemed to hold his weight. Slowly, Erick pulled his leg out from the freezing water. Again, he clearly imagined the ice giving way completely and his body being pulled beneath the water. Erick was in the most trouble he'd been in during his short life. Now that his leg was out, he had to move slowly in order to prevent the web-like cracks from rupturing. He knew death would be certain if he moved too fast or in the wrong direction.

With his leg out of the ice tomb, he began to feel the numbness settle into it. He shuddered as he heard a deafening crack. *Oh God, no. I'm going down with no one to save me; no one to even know where I am,* he thought. His mind raced along at breakneck speed. He wondered if he'd be missed. Who would miss him first? Who would miss him the most? He had no time to answer his own questions. The abrupt sound of another loud crack beneath him interrupted his thoughts. He didn't fall through, but the image of himself clinging to the edge of the ice hole and the cold ice water sucking at his clothing flashed across his mind. Those thoughts snapped him back to the reality of his problem.

He thought if he lay down across the ice to spread his weight out, he would have a better chance of successfully crawling across the web-like cracks. His sled was only twenty-five yards away and with it, dry clothing, boots, and plenty of matches to start a fire. Suddenly he heard the deep haunting sounds of wolves and he knew they were hunting. Erick had been so engrossed with saving his life that he hadn't noticed the darkness that had crept over the creek. It was now nightfall and the wolves were hunting for dinner. Erick would be the main course unless he got off that platter of ice.

As one wolf howled, another would answer. The blackness of the night came alive with the evening howls of the killers. Erick had to crawl across the ice to get to the creek's edge. Crawling prone on his belly, cradling his rifle, and dragging his partially frozen right leg behind him sounded plausible. Rethinking the fact that he was dragging a weighted-down right leg and foot, which felt like a block of ice, made him stop. He looked down the hole in the ice and realized exactly what had happened. He could see a large space between the top of the water's surface and the underside of the ice. The constantly moving creek water had hollowed out the ice in the center of the creek. The ice Erick had chopped out at the creek's edge was four inches thick, but the ice from the water's movement had hollowed to a thin two inches at the center of the creek. Erick was now lying on ice that was only two inches thick.

The snow had never slowed while Erick had been fighting for his life. It also seemed as if the wind had picked up a bit and was now blowing straight down the mouth of the creek. Overhead, he could hear the whisper of the wind through the tops of the tall pines. But there was something else he heard. The sound was the movement of wings. He could hear it above the pines, but the darkness and falling snow prevented him from seeing any further. Erick looked up through the snow that was cascading down on his weakened body. Suddenly he saw what he had heard; an adult bald eagle was circling above him. It almost knew that the young trapper was slowly dying and it waited to be first to stake out its kill. The eagle was truly the vulture of the north. Eagles were known to mark their kill and stay with it until late at night. They would roost on their kill and would slowly tear at its flesh while it was still alive, ripping pieces of succulent meat loose and swallowing them whole.

Erick turned his thoughts away from the eagle and proceeded to think of a way off of the ice island. Erick lay flat on his belly and stared straight ahead at the distance he would have to crawl. He started, ever slowly, moving forward an inch at a time, dragging his right leg behind him. His pants and boots were frozen together as one. Just then the ice cracked again. With that, there came a deep-throated howl from the woods. He knew the howl wasn't the cougar, but he thought it could be the Namekagan. He wondered if they had been tracking him all this time, just waiting for the perfect moment to attack. Erick knew that moment would be now. His mind raced along wondering what would get to him first: the ice-cold black water, the cougar silently waiting his chance, or possibly the Namekagan. The one most likely to enjoy Erick, sooner or later, would be the eagle, whether now or in the spring when his body would be exposed to the world, floating aimlessly down Potato Creek.

Again, there was the howl from the woods. Maybe it wasn't the Namekagan, but only a lonely wolf. This time, the sound seemed to come almost from on the ice. Erick remained silent and as still as a fawn standing next to its mother. There was no movement from Erick, not even his eyebrow twitched. At this point he thought it really didn't matter who or what would get him first. Tears welled up in Erick's eyes. *If only I hadn't crossed the creek,* he thought. He thought of his mother first and then his father. He wanted either one right now to give him some sign, some idea of what to do.

Then Erick recalled sitting at a campfire his father had built one summer night. His father had taken Erick along to teach him, as his father would say, "the ways of the woods." His father told a story of a hunter a long time ago. This hunter had a disastrous tale to tell, similar to Erick's. As the story went, the hunter was walking across one of the thousands of lakes in Sweden and deep into a harsh cold winter. The lake ice was thick, almost six inches, so there wasn't any danger of the ice cracking. The hunter was tracking a trophy elk that must have weighed four hundred pounds and had a rack of sixteen points. The hunter gave no thought to the ice cracking, because the buck weighed more than he did. The ice had been strong enough to hold the buck's four hoofs, but the weight distribution of the hunter was condensed into a smaller area.

As the story went, the hunter heard the ice cracking under his weight. Thinking quickly, he laid down on the cracking ice. He spread out his arms and legs as if to make snow angels. This action spread his full body weight out over a larger area. The hunter threw his rifle way off to the side and carefully unbuttoned his knapsack with his store of food and threw that off to the side also. The hunter moved, but as he did the ice cracked. He then held perfectly still for what seemed to have been an hour. Then, very slowly, he began to crawl, but once again the ice started to crack. The hunter knew he was in big trouble. He knew falling into the frozen cold lake water could be a certain and swift death. After waiting a long time, the hunter decided on a plan of action that could save him from the watery grave below him. He decided to wait. He waited through the day, lying motionless. The day passed and darkness came swiftly. He looked up at the sky full of stars and the moon that shown down on the cracked ice. The hunter knew that the night would bring the deep cold to be expected during that time of winter.

The night grew extremely cold. He could hear the ice cracking, but cracking in a good way. The ice was crystallizing and becoming stronger as it bonded tightly together. The hunter figured it to be one or two in the morning and he thought that the ice would be strong enough for him to crawl toward shore. He started to move forward only to find that his arms and legs, still in the spread eagle position, were frozen to the ice. His clothing had frozen to the surface of the lake. It seemed that the warm afternoon temperatures along with his warm body heat had allowed the ice directly beneath him to melt a little. As the lake refroze, his wet clothing froze tightly to the ice. The hunter was trapped onto the lake's surface with his clothing holding him rigid. He was now a permanent part of the lake.

Erick did not want to think any longer about his father's story. Erick thought if he lay prone like the hunter in the story, he wouldn't make the hunter's mistake. Erick made his decision quickly. He would lay prone, spread eagle like a snow angel, except that he would cut off the buttons from his shirt and his coat. He felt that if he became frozen to the ice, at least he would be able to break free from his loose-fitting clothing. He also took his hunting knife out of its sheath and laid it close to his right hand. He decided to wait as long as he could before cutting off the buttons.

His night on the ice went slowly. He didn't hear the eagle's wings again all night. No Namekagan men rushed across the ice to devour him and no cougar or wolf raced headlong across the ice to snap his neck in one quick and violent lunge. Dawn was on Erick before he knew night had ended. The day started bright and sunny. It was time to make his move. He started to get up but found, like the hunter in his fathers story, that his clothing had become frozen into the ice. With his buttons removed he simply slipped out of his clothing but he did have to cut one of his pant legs off with his hunting knife.

Erick picked up his rifle and proceeded to crawl off the ice. "So far, so good," he mumbled. Inch by inch, foot by foot, he crawled along pulling his right leg behind him. His crawling ended as he finally reached the shore's embankment and one of his beaver stakes.

Erick was safe, or so he thought. He crawled up the embankment to the sled, picked up his extra pants, boots, and matches. Slitting his pants, he removed them completely exposing his numb leg. *Doesn't look too good,* he thought. He cut off his right boot. The sight of his foot frightened him a little. It was pale blue in color and was numb to the touch. He slid on his replacement socks, dry long underwear, and other clothes. Already, a new warmth came into his leg. It was now only early morning.

Erick started a fire using his dry matches from the sled. The fire soon began to crackle and pop. It only took a few moments to get a roaring fire going. He sat in front of the fire massaging his right leg gently. He continued to hobble over and put more wood onto the blaze. He flexed his foot and felt movement in his toes, but his foot was still tender when he put his full weight onto it. He wanted to start back to his camp but knew he couldn't, at least not yet. He sat by the roaring fire, hour after hour. As each hour passed, his leg and foot felt better and better.

He put more wood on the fire and thought about the predators in the woods and sky. He had nothing at all to worry about right now, not even the sound of distant howling. Erick had one dandy campfire going as he continued to cut wood with his ax. The flames leaped high into the afternoon sky. He was so tired from his all-night ordeal. That coupled with the heat from his blazing fire made his eyes begin to close.

Erick awoke with a start. His fire had gone out and the shadows from the forest had started to creep upon his temporary camp. He had been sitting on the edge of his sled with his head resting on his folded arms that were propped up on his knees. As he moved to get up, he simply fell over into the wet melted snow. Both his legs had gone to sleep. After a few moments, circulation began to rush through his legs again. He was fine, but he felt more exhausted than when he fell into his well-deserved sleep.

Woodsmen never know the correct time, day or night, but as close as he could tell it was 6:00 in the evening. His campfire was almost completely out except for a few glowing embers. He broke down the fire and separated any wood that still had a glow or was smoldering. Erick had no food or coffee on the sled, so as quickly as he could, he strapped down his traps, picked up his rifle, and was on his way back to his main camp. He'd had enough of this creek mouth. The young trapper felt lucky just to be alive. He thought to himself, *I'll be back tomorrow but I'll have a far better day than this one has been.*

It didn't take Erick more than a couple of hours to get back to his base camp. When he arrived, he was pleased to find it as he had left it. First, he pulled on the rope that held his food sack high up in the poplar tree. Hunters and trappers always kept their food stocks high up in a tree, far from the reach of nosy, pesky animals. The worst animal to pillage had always been the black bear, but there was no sense worrying about those critters because they were all in hibernation this time of year.

It had been more than thirty-six hours since Erick had eaten and he was starved half to death. He first cut himself two generous slices of elk steak and portioned out an ample amount of beans. Cutting through his mother's frozen bread took some effort. It was like cutting through a block of ice with a knife. His campfire came up and alive fast with the dry kindling he had cut days before. The elk simmered in the pan and the beans smelled like they were heavensent. Erick put four pieces of his mother's bread on a hickory stick and held them over the flickering flames until they were golden brown. He then opened a container of his mother's homemade apple butter, suspended it over the flames to unthaw, then quickly smeared it heavily onto the thick slices of golden bread. His pot of coffee was hot and smelled great. Elk steak, beans, homemade bread, and coffee filled his empty stomach and gave him the energy boost he so dearly needed.

Finishing his meal, he looked around and heard absolutely nothing coming from the forest. He felt this was not right, as the forest always makes sounds of some sort. Erick saw nothing to alarm himself and realized it was too early to go to bed, plus he was wide-awake after his big meal. He decided to cut some kindling for breakfast in the morning. He also cut some branches to make a spit across his campfire; after all, he had every intention of shooting himself some fresh meat for dinner. With that thought in mind and a full feeling deep in his stomach, he simply sat down and closed his eyes.

It was some time later when he suddenly awoke and noticed that he was not alone anymore. There it was about a hundred yards off to his right staring right back at him. It was dinner. Well, it was possibly dinner, but not quite yet. It was a bright red fox with a black tip on his tail and black leggings. Erick thought for a minute about taking aim on this beautiful animal. His stomach was full from the big dinner and he still had a lot of food left in his food sack. He thought long and hard and finally decided another big meal could wait. Anyway, if he shot the fox, the pelt wouldn't be worth hardly anything. He decided to wait and possibly catch it in his trap. And with that, the fox briskly hopped away like an overgrown rabbit, but so gracefully. The fox looked so elegant against the backdrop of snow as he slowly ambled out of sight. It looked like it might be heading toward Erick's traps.

In December 1885, Erick reflected on what an experience he was having. He wondered if anyone was thinking about him as night settled on his little camp. He gathered more wood, cut it down to a reasonable size, and continued to chop until his arms ached. There would be plenty of wood to keep his fire hot and bright through the night with lots left over for breakfast. He added more to the fire, looked over his little bit of heaven, thanked God for saving his life, then covered himself with two of his warm woolen blankets, and fell deep into a well-needed sleep.

Erick slept restlessly. He dreamt of ice, danger, and the ending of his father's story of the hunter, locked to the lake ice. The rest of the story, the part he had refused to think about while awake, came out in his dreams. The hunter's body had melted the ice beneath him, freezing him tight to the lake's surface. The hunter couldn't free himself no matter how hard he tried. He was caught like a moth in a spider web. The hunter screamed for help from anyone. But who would hear his screams out on the empty body of lake ice? No other hunters were out and certainly no travelers were passing through. He finally gave up calling for help from sheer exhaustion. He fell fast asleep.

At what must have been three or four in the morning, the hunter was awakened by some sound. He lay motionless, first opening one eye slightly and then the other. He lifted his head only inches to see what the sound had been. Just then there was a distant howl from the lake's edge and the forest's start. He noticed that the overcast sky had disappeared and had been replaced while he slept with a bright full moon. *Just my luck,* the hunter thought. *I must stick out like a boulder in a stream.* Another howl cut the cold clear night, and then another. This time, the howls seemed somewhat closer and behind him. He couldn't turn his body far enough to see. The howling grew closer and more frightening. He looked over at his rifle, which was only three yards away. He tried once again to break free from the icy grip of the lake but couldn't. The hunter screamed out as loud as he could. He saw the forest shadows moving relentlessly toward him, as if the forest would suffocate his very soul.

Suddenly, he could make out the difference between trees and shadows and the dark outline of a wolf against the bright white snow. The wolf was moving closer across the snow-covered lake. Again, he looked over at his rifle. Just at that moment, he saw a second and third moving shadow coming out of the forest's edge and onto the open snow of the lake. The wolves were now trotting across the lake's moonlit surface. He counted seven. They didn't seem to be slowing down, even as he screamed for help. The wolves were close enough now for the hunter to make out their coloring. The wolves were led by a darkened black, followed by a brown and then by a gray wolf. They all seemed to be suffering from the mange. They were all filthy and dirty looking. He thought, *What, no time to bathe before dinner?*

He yelled and screamed at the top of his lungs until no more sounds came out. The pack didn't slow down. He saw another pack coming from the tree line and running full speed as if someone was ringing a dinner bell at his feet. The hunter quickly realized that these were two separate packs of wolves. A light gray or possibly dirty white leader led the second pack. They were overtaking the first pack, which was still cautiously moving toward him. They were close enough now for him to see their yellow eyes, their flattened down ears, and the fur standing straight out, away from their bodies.

They were so close now that the hunter could smell the foul odor coming from their unkempt bodies. There was a smell of death upon their filthy, matted down coats. These were devil dogs, made up from the meanest animals of the Swedish North Woods. They were survivors of the fittest wolf families and they would kill, without any hesitation, anything and everything that crossed their paths. They had to kill for survival. The hunter could see their haunting yellow devil eyes, white teeth flashing as if forcing a smile, and what seemed like dozens of pinkish tongues hanging from open, panting mouths.

They all bore down on the helpless hunter, snarling and yipping as they drowned out his last high-pitched screams. Tearing at his clothing and ripping at his soft, warm flesh, all sounds were silenced as a female leader crushed the hunter's neck in her vise-like grip. No more sounds came from the hunter. The only sounds heard were the sounds of meat being ripped from bone and long red tongues slurping up blood as it sprayed up out of shredded veins torn clean from the body. The pure white snow had turned crimson red in a pool of blood surrounding the hunter's remains. The wolf pack feasted throughout the night, leaving nothing but bones and clothing.

Erick awoke and bolted straight up out of his warm woolen blankets, his body covered with wet, warm sweat. He didn't like his father's story when he first told it and liked it even less as he relived it a second time in his dream.

Dawn was approaching and early morning rays of light bled through the eastern tree line. Erick's stomach growled as if to say, "Feed me, feed me." His fire was only a memory. He knew hard work was waiting for him. The fire came up fast and with it came warmth. His morning coffee seemed better today than it had on previous days.

After a big breakfast, Erick cut additional kindling and covered it with his canvas to save it for evening. Erick packed up his sled, tied his food up in the poplar tree, and started out toward the mouth of Potato Creek to make a second attempt at setting his traps. This newly seasoned trapper would not be walking across the creek this time.

Erick moved cautiously along the edge of the creek. He walked half a mile downstream. He then chopped a decent size hole through the ice and lowered his baited beaver trap down the hole, driving his stake into and through six inches of ice. Up ahead, he noticed some open water out toward the creek's center. No way was he going near the potential danger, so he climbed back onto the shore and pulled his sled far beyond the open water. This young and now well-experienced trapper knew that there must have been a sizable spring to have so much open water out in front of him.

After passing the open water at a safe distance, Erick turned around in time to see ten to twelve geese fly in to land on the water. Erick knew that those geese and goslings were most likely a whole family that he might have seen the previous summer. Families of geese always stayed together for the first full year. He thought about the fact that, when a new brood is about to be born, the parents chase away the year-old goslings in a not so polite manner.

Erick chopped another hole in the ice for yet another beaver trap, but all the time he thought of the geese swimming on the spring's open water. As usual, Erick had grown hungry and the hungrier he got the more he wanted a succulent goose dinner. All this time, Erick had kept his back to the screaming geese that seemed to think the open water was their own backyard swimming hole. He kept his distance because he knew the geese could suddenly become vicious and attack him if they figured they could win in a fight. Just the thought of that was the last straw for Erick. He picked up his rifle off of the sled, took careful aim and fired. The noise from the shot was deafening. The closest goose simply slumped over and was about to become Erick's dinner. He carefully climbed down the embankment but couldn't quite reach the dead goose. He quickly cut a long birch sapling and pulled the goose over to the edge of ice. His lips were watering from memories of his mother preparing many goose dinners for the family.

He threw his future dinner onto the sled and again proceeded to pull his sled along the creek's edge. Erick continued to lay out his trap line for another five miles. Ravens seemed to follow him every step of the way. They were surely the most annoying birds in the whole country. But Erick also knew that if the ravens ever quieted down their constant chattering, it meant he was not alone any longer. Knowing this fact, he was happy that they were so loud. They were on almost every tree branch above Erick's head. Who knows, maybe they had been friends with the dead goose on his sled?

Erick continued to chop his holes and set his traps. Finally in late afternoon he drove his last stake into the frozen tundra, which accounted for forty-six traps. He had set all the traps he had taken with him. He was very tired but realized he, Erick the Trapper, had done a man's job. Now with his sled almost empty except for some clothing, his rifle, and the goose, he began to pull his sled back to camp. It was a lot easier going back with an empty sled than when he began with a fully loaded sled. He was almost up to the open water where the geese were. To his amazement, they had returned, minus the one on Erick's sled, of course. The geese surely remembered Erick because they all began screeching and honking as Erick came into view. They finally took off and flew straight down the creek, away from Erick's direction of travel.

It didn't seem to take long for Erick to make his way back into camp. Everything looked all right as he placed the sled under an old spruce. Walking over to his campfire, long extinguished by the dozen hours he had been away, he discovered fresh, crisp animal prints in the snow. "Oh, God, now what?" he exclaimed. "Who the devil was this intruder?" This puzzle was easy to solve. He could tell from the four toes and large pad on each of its four feet that it must be a lynx, not uncommon in the Lotorp wilderness. They were no danger at all, according to his father.

Erick looked toward the woods where the tracks led but saw nothing. He turned toward the creek and looked up the embankment. There, standing at the top of the embankment, was the lynx. The cat simply stood across the creek staring Erick down. It seemed as if the cat was daring Erick to come across the creek after him. Erick wasn't about to commit that deadly sin again. *No midnight swim for me, thank you,* Erick thought to himself.

The lynx appeared quite statuesque standing on top of the embankment with the moon popping in and out behind it. Father had said that the lynx was a short tailed, long legged wildcat. Erick thought back to his father's schooling him in the ways of the woods. Father had said, "Don't be confused, as the lynx is similar in appearance to the bobcat.

Lynx are larger and have longer ear tufts." Erick knew that this was a lynx and not a bobcat due to its black tipped tail. It looked to be about three feet long and possibly weighed thirty-five pounds. Erick remembered Father saying that the lynx had retractable claws for fighting, climbing rock ledges and trees. He also said that their large feet act like snow-shoes, enabling them to walk easily on the surface of deep snow. Oh, yes, this was a lynx for sure.

The cat stared at Erick, as if he had never seen a human boy before. It didn't look like this confrontation was going anyplace and cat and boy stood eyeball to eyeball without moving. Finally Erick had enough. "These are my woods. Move on, if you would, please," Erick hollered. With that unconditional threat, the lynx walked off into the woods. Erick didn't think he would be having any trouble from the lynx, so he too moved on.

There was total darkness now and Erick had to get a fire started to cook his goose. His father was always right. He always told him to cut his evening firewood early in the morning. He uncovered his buried treasure trove of dry fire-wood and within minutes Erick had himself a roaring fire. He put on the coffee and then cleaned the goose. After cleaning the goose, he put it on a skewer and placed it over the fire. Goose grease dripped continuously onto the flames below. It did not take too long to turn a golden brown. He started a few biscuits in a pan and pulled out his mother's apple butter. His beans heated quickly and the goose not long after. Everything tasted fabulous. Of course, the goose was succulent and filled his growling, empty stomach. He thought it had to be the best dinner of his life.

Erick was full, almost to the bursting point. He began his chores of cleaning his coffeepot and cooking pans with fresh clean snow, using the washcloth Mother had packed for this occasion. Tired as he was, he began the evening ritual of cutting firewood for the next fire. Erick had been lucky that the temperature held comfortably at freezing or slightly below freezing. He sat down with a clear head, brought on by the fine, solid dinner. He started thinking of the mysterious animal tracks he had seen. *Could be a beaver,* he thought, knowing that they, on some occasions, came up away from their watery lodges. *But if it had been a beaver, then there would be the markings of its tail dragging through the snow,* he reasoned. *It could also be a porcupine or raccoon, but they're both hibernating along with the black bear. Then again, it could be a black bear awakened by a hunter crashing through the brush or loggers dropping a tree on their winter lodge.* After a short deliberation, he put the mystery to rest, determining that it was, in fact, a lynx.

Erick felt this was a poor time for his mind to be going down the alphabet of animals. He decided to call it a day and covered himself so as to be warm through the night. His fire was high, but to play it safe, he pulled his rifle in under his blankets and removed the safety latch. "Can't be too careful out here alone," he mumbled to himself. With that thought, Erick fell fast asleep. For the first time since leaving home, he rested peacefully. It could have been a number of things: sheer exhaustion, a filling dinner, contentment in his own camp, or sleeping with his rifle cradled in his arms. It really didn't matter what the reason was for such a long and restful sleep. Erick was long overdue to have the peaceful sleep of a seven-year-old.

Erick was firmly locked in the middle of a solid six months of winter, six months of frozen, icy hell. He dreamt of summer when the sun broke open early and stayed late after bed. Long evening shadows would engulf the backwoods cabin he called home. Creating the hand-hewn logs for the cabin seemed like an impossibly daunting task. They had been put together like a pyramid, layer upon layer, until they reached the roof joists. The cabin was nearly invisible, resting at the base of giant and stately jack pines. Light breezes would blow the sweet smell of the pines and would drift heavily across his nose. He dreamed of the warmth back home in his cabin. It would be so warm, in fact, that he would run around in his underclothes. His father would be resting in a chair with his back and chest wrapped tightly from the terrible fall he had taken months before. Erick's nose sniffed the air beneath the blankets, imagining the smell of fresh apple pies that his mother had taken out of the fireplace. With that fresh in his mind, he awoke. He came to the quick realization that there was no apple pie and certainly no warm cabin, and oh, was it cold. His fire had gone out, most likely hours before.

He peered out of his temporary shelter of pine boughs and poplar branches. A fluffy white snow was falling. Erick did not bound out of his bed of leaves and thick pine needles. He didn't throw back his blankets and leap out of his warm snug bed. No, his little body just wanted to be a little boy once again. For just a little while longer, Erick wanted to remain a seven-year-old, going on eight. If only for a few more minutes, he wanted to remain within the cradle of protection, protected from the cold and snow, the freezing creek water, and all the forest animals that seemed to remain in the forefront of his mind. He remained under the warm blankets for just a little while longer.

Erick lay there and thought of all the excitement of growing up on the farm. Every day there would be a new learning experience. He remembered the day Father came running at full speed into the cabin, so excited. "Mother," he had hollered, even though she was standing but five feet away. "Why he calls my mother, Mother, I will never understand," Erick mused. "Mother," he exclaimed again,

"Martha, she's having a calf. Quickly, heat some water, gather towels, hurry. Erick, you can help, too." Mother filled the kettle with water and swung the filled kettle over the hearth on its swivel that Father had made up in the barn. Erick stayed with Mother, helping her gather items needed to help in the birthing of the calf. They were all so very excited about Martha giving birth. The water heated quickly after Mother added more wood. She said, "Erick, you carry the towels and I will carry the hot kettle up to the barn." They both hurried up to help with the birthing, even little Charles followed along behind his mother.

There lay Martha, right inside the barn door, howling at the top of her lungs. All Erick could see was two of Martha's legs as he held onto his mother's leg and peered around her large frame. Slowly, appearing out from between Martha's legs, came what appeared to be a calf. Mother whispered, "Not too close Erick. Give her plenty of room. She may kick and you could get hurt." Father wet a towel and rubbed Martha's forehead with it. Martha gave a loud moo, which may have meant, "Thanks, Pa, thanks a lot."

Father kept talking to Martha as if the cow could understand. Martha pushed harder and harder. Soon the whole calf emerged. Mother and Father both worked together to clean up and wash the calf with the warm towels, paying little attention to Martha. The calf was beautiful in a sort of messy, slimy, and bloody way. Father said she was a Holstein, a milk cow, like her mother. Looking down at this fragile delicate little animal, it all seemed like a miracle. It would certainly be a long time before his family got any milk from the little girl. The calf struggled to her feet. She just stood there, rocking and wobbling on her tiny little legs until she just fell over on her side. What a thrill to be part of such a wonderful experience as seeing life begin.

At that very moment Father screamed out, "Martha's not moving." No sounds came from her. Father felt her side but could detect no movement. He gave her a hard and solid punch to the ribs but still nothing. Father was desperate, as this was their only cow, their only opportunity to enjoy the benefits of milk every day and freshly churned butter. Father gave Martha another fierce punch to her chest. Still no reaction, no motion, no breath of air, no heartbeat. He began to beat his fist on her chest as hard as he could, but there was still nothing. He ran over to the opposite side of the barn and ran back across the straw covered floor. Father never ran that fast and that hard before. He crashed into Martha's side as hard as he could. Martha let out an enormous belch, her heart began to beat, and her sides started moving in and out. She gave a tremendous moo and tried to stagger up onto her feet. She rolled this way and that way, back and forth, but still couldn't quite get up.

Father said, "We have to get her up fast or she may not recover." He pushed a heavy rope under her backside. Then he hooked it to a beam above. He then hooked his block and tackle up to the beam. This was followed by hooking a come-along winch to the rope and hollering for Erick to tighten the come-along. A "come-along" was a rope and two pulleys connected to a permanent structure which, when connected to a heavy movable object with a gearing mechanism, winched the movable object with little effort. They winched the ropes tight around Martha and began to raise her slowly. The barn beam groaned and began to bend downward, threatening to snap. Martha groaned louder than the barn beam. Father yelled, "Erick, run over to your mother and little Charles and stay put."

They all looked up at the beam, expecting it to crack and split any minute. Martha weighed close to two thousand pounds, so the beam cracking was a real possibility. Mother looked up at the beam while Father tended the come-along. The beam held and didn't break. Martha gave an earth-shattering howl as the rope tightened around her backside and her hoofs were kicking as she tried to stand up. Suddenly, she was standing on all four legs. Martha was solidly on the barn floor and looked steady enough for Father to release the ropes that held her tight. Father cut the binding rope loose and, for the first time, Martha looked at her newborn calf. It looked as if a smile came over Martha's face as she looked in approvingly at her baby girl. The calf walked over to her mother, with her shaky little wobbly legs and began nursing from Martha. Erick had been grateful for the happy ending to a nearly tragic birthing event.

CHAPTER THREE

Erick ever so slowly pulled the three woolen blankets off and leaped to his feet. The blankets had been like a dead weight on his sixty-eight pound body, but they had kept Erick extremely warm throughout the night.

Erick could see a light snow falling beyond his shelter. He peered out into the white winter wonderland that he had ignored for days. *Such a beautiful place, the Lotorp forest,* he thought. *Certainly there could not be a more beautiful place in all of Sweden.*

The peaceful morning air was broken by a far distant howl of a wolf. Erick propped his rifle up against his stack of firewood and proceeded to start his breakfast fire. Only moments later he had a rip-roaring fire blazing away. He rubbed his hands together over the soaring flames. He could feel the warmth coming up in his body. *Oh,* he thought, *this will be my finest day.* Today he would try to set a few snares for ruffed grouse. Just the thought of grouse cooking on his spit suspended over an open fire made Erick's mouth water.

After breakfast, Erick packed his second sled, which was much smaller than his trapping sled. After loading snares, bait, ax, and rifle, he was on his way.

For the first time since he had left his cabin and family, he felt good about everything. He hadn't gone but a hundred yards when he abruptly stopped. He saw fresh tracks in the snow. He had slept so deeply during the night that he hadn't heard any animals. These were tracks most common in Sweden. They belonged to an elk. Erick stood quietly as the haunting sounds of the bull elk bugled across the Lotorp forest. This was elk country and he was aware that the bull elk was now trumpeting behind a stand of high pines. *Lucky day, huh? We will see just how lucky this day is going to be,* thought Erick.

Fog began to drift into the lake area from the low tamarack bogs. The early morning sun was just beginning to rise behind the thick black forest. Erick was down close to the lake's thick southern swampland, but the swampland was still in a deep dark sleep from nightfall. There had been a solid, heavy frost during the night, and the trees and snow-covered trail glistened brightly in the predawn light. Mother Nature was putting on her finest performance.

A hair-raising bugling came echoing across the woods, followed by another bugling. Erick's heart nearly pounded his other organs half to death and almost came to a complete stop. The hair on his arms stood straight up. All in the forest grew quiet as a grave. Now, frightened out of his skin, he heard heavy hoofs pounding into the thick frost layer. Through the thick fog, he saw steam rising like a geyser into the heavy fog-filled air. Many elk were stampeding through the underbrush and crushing and tearing the bushes loose with their massive antlers. He heard continuing bugling as the cow elks and yearling calves were running just out of his sight. He could hear the thick brush around him snapping like kindling on a hot fire as these massive animals came closer and closer to him. Blindly punching their way through the fog-darkened thickness of the darkest timber, these vegetation-eating giants were like bulls in a china shop. The sounds of their outstretched antlers slicing through the undergrowth made Erick shudder from top to bottom. Behind Erick came a bull elk. The snow and fog had tricked Erick; he had thought the sounds of the elk herd were coming from off to the east, but here the bull elk stood, so majestic and so frighteningly intimidating.

Erick looked closely. There was a cloud of fog and steam created by the bull's breath circling around the bull's head. His enormous antlers glimmered brightly in the dawn's early sunlight as he gave yet another bugle. The bull bugled and bugled and bugled until Erick's eardrums rang like a bell and he thought he had gone deaf.

Erick just stood there frozen in time. The bull elk's front right hoof pounded the snow-covered earth. This was the largest bull elk Erick had ever witnessed. None of Father's stories could come close to what Erick was experiencing first-hand at that moment. He couldn't believe he was standing in front of this magnificent animal, the true king of the woods. With all his incredible power and strength, the bull was nothing short of intimidating. Through the fog, Erick could see, one by one, that the bull's wilderness harem of cows was following their fearless leader and mentor. About ten cows and ten calves emerged into the clearing on the other side of the creek. By now, Erick had taken deep cover behind a massive red oak that had fallen many years earlier from a lightening strike. The fallen oak completely hid young Erick from the frightening dark eyes of the bull. The bull looked in Erick's direction toward the lightening struck log. Again the bull broke the quiet of the forest by letting out another frightening bugling sound.

Erick didn't dare peek over the fallen log for fear of being seen. He could envision the bull lowering his head, stomping his hoofs, and charging him with those enormous, majestic antlers. He could envision the bull crashing across the frozen creek in a single bound and goring him to death with those glistening antlers. *Not exactly the way one would like to die,* he thought. Right now it seemed a real possibility, but as Erick's luck would have it, the bull looked away and angrily threw his head back and forth in defiance of anything and everything. The bull simply walked off down toward Potato Lake with his harem of cows cowering slowly behind at a safe distance.

When Erick knew he was completely safe and out of danger, he slowly raised himself up from behind the fallen red oak. He tried to visualize the magnitude of the danger he had just escaped. He stood there for a moment and thanked God, once again, for saving him from what could have been his last breath.

With the danger from the bull and his cows temporarily removed from his mind, Erick continued to pull his sled along the creek. He came to an area of heavy, low-lying brush and decided to set a snare for grouse. He followed that up with a second snare about a thousand yards ahead and then a third and fourth where he thought grouse might cross the area. With all his snares baited and set he walked back to camp to cut firewood and kindling. He was anticipating a well-deserved grouse feast.

Erick decided that he would leave after breakfast the next morning to check the traps he had set around Potato Lake and to figure out how he would haul all his beaver, fox, and mink on his sleds. His father had told him to find a secure location that would be accessible so they could come back in the spring to pick up all the traps, the ax, and Swede saw. He envisioned his sleds piled high with a full week's bounty.

Erick ate an early dinner of baking powder biscuits to give him energy. Then he headed out to check his grouse snares. No grouse were in the first two snares or the third. Now Erick was getting worried that he might not get his mouth-watering grouse dinner, thinking it may only have been a fantasy. On discovering that his last snare too was empty, Erick headed back to camp hungry and dejected.

He decided to go back over his plan to leave early in the morning to check his traps. Erick thought nothing could get any worse than all those empty snares. Tomorrow he would triumph by retrieving his trapped bounty from along his trap line. All that his father and grandfather had taught him would be put into play.

Erick slept a hungry and restless night, tossing and turning, worrying and wondering about his trap line. He dreamt of muskrats, mink, otter, fox, raccoon, ermine, and that old codger, "Mister Beaver." He dreamt about his father telling him that expertise at trapping comes quickly to those with a keen sense of observation. He had told Erick that others could wander the woods forever and miss the many little telltale details that make a trapper successful.

Over the summer, Father had trained Erick how to find good locations for setting traps. Erick knew where there were plenty of beaver by observing the number of trees felled. Secondly, he could tell by the bark eaten from the aspens, poplars, alders, and willows. By these signs, he knew he was in the heartland of the beaver. The rodents had dammed Potato Creek to make their pond. He could see their lodge protruding up through the ice. Father had explained that they build canals and runways to move building materials and create a cache. The beaver lodge was close to six feet high and fifteen feet in diameter. In the lodge, Erick knew it was common to find numerous family groups including their kits. Erick trained himself to see and analyze all the little evidences left by the furbearers.

In the summer months, Erick would go to the closest creek with an exposed beaver lodge and sit and observe. Quietly and unnoticed, he would watch and learn the many little secrets of the beaver. He would watch them up on the opposite shore hauling rocks and using their large flat tails for balance. While swimming, they used their tails as rudders to help while hauling large branches used to constantly redesign and modify their lodges as individual family condos. Erick would watch with amazement as the little kits joined their parents in the engineering and building of the lodges. Sadly, though, the kits would be driven off after their second year to start their own life. The male and female beavers joined for life and had an average of four kits a year.

Father had taught him not to trap or kill furbearers until their fur was prime or they would be cheated of top prices for the pelts. Father described pelts that were not properly skinned, fleshed, stretched, and dried. He also told Erick that each captured furbearer on his trap line had to be skinned on the spot, rolled, and wrapped and then placed carefully on the sleds. In addition, once Erick brought home the pelts, they would have to be stretched onto drying boards. Father had drying boards of all kinds and sizes out in the barn. The boards had to be in proportion to the size of the animals. Father explained that if the skins were improperly dried, they would be an eyesore and lack trimness. He said overstretching would show up thin spots that should be pinched.

Erick remembered the day Father had given him his personalized skinning knife for his seventh birthday. The knife was a prime requisite for the art of pelting. Father's knife was equipped with a slitting blade for general use. The blades were protected in an oilskin sheath to keep them keen and sharp. A dull blade would cause more damage to pelts than a sharp blade that did its job smoothly and without friction. Erick remembered every word his father had told him on trapping. Erick retained all that he had learned on preparing pelts in order to receive the highest value for each one.

Erick awoke in a cold sweat. He felt the responsibility that had been placed upon him. He knew it was time to reap the benefits of his labors by collecting his pelts.

It had begun to snow. *Perfect day,* he thought jokingly. He ate a quick breakfast from his rapidly depleting food stock. He pulled his sleds behind him, making sure he had plenty of binding and ropes to tie the contents of his traps onto the sleds. One sled would be used for retrieving traps and the other for the meat and pelts.

The continuing snow made pulling the sleds harder and harder. After a tough walk through much higher snow than when he had set the traps, he reached his first trap in the creek's ice. He had to chop a hole through the ice that had formed during the days since he'd set the trap. Erick pulled his trap chain up through the hole in the ice. The dark image of a beaver floated up with the trap chain through the clear cold water. Erick's heart pumped a mile a minute. Total exhilaration flooded his body at the thought of having trapped his first beaver. Father and Grandfather would burst their buttons with pride to be here watching Erick bringing in his first beaver.

As Erick raised the trap up through the chopped hole, his eyes widened like saucers and his mouth opened wide. His lungs were so emptied of breath that no sound came from his now trembling body. There, before Erick's eyes, dangling on his trap chain was, he thought, a beaver. But any resemblance to a beaver was not to be found. It looked as if a lumberjack had chopped it to death with his double-sided ax. Blood covered it completely. Gaping holes were exposed where beautiful fur had once been. Erick still held the chain up in front of him at eye level looking desperately for where the animal's head had once been. Unable to tell one end from the other, he threw the carcass down in the snow.

Tears flowed down Erick's face. How could anyone or anything mutilate this once beautiful animal? He couldn't look at it any longer. He left it lying in the snow along with the trap and chain. He just couldn't bring himself to touch it and release it from the trap. He cleansed his hands in the cold creek water of his chopped hole and decided to move on toward his next trap.

CHAPTER FOUR

Erick stopped abruptly and reconsidered. He couldn't leave one of God's creatures lying out on the snow for the world to see and the wolves to eat. He couldn't bury it due to the three-foot frostline, so he decided to throw it onto his sled, still connected to the trap and chain. There it was done. He bound it to the sled. It was a sickening sight. The animal looked as if it had been turned inside out. Erick quickly looked away from the carcass.

He remembered his father telling him that, when he returned, all Erick's furs would be shipped to Europe where finery made from prime skinned mammals was all the rage. The fur from this animal wouldn't be used that way.

There was a blood-curdling howl from a distant wolf, which was most likely watching Erick's every move. The howl was no doubt angry because Erick was taking the wolf's dinner away on the sled. Erick looked up briefly, but then pulled his sled on toward his next trap around the following bend.

Erick saw his second stake protruding through the snow. Once again he knelt down, pushed the snow out of the way, and began to chop away at the newly formed ice. Success! He saw the dark shadow of a beaver attached solidly to his trap. The beaver was still and motionless as a tomb, so he began to lift it up to the surface.

Erick froze in place as the water hole filled with blood from the beaver. Father never explained that there would be so much blood. Erick pulled the trap chain up through the hole and was shocked at what he saw. Something or some-one had attacked the beaver. The beaver's fur had been rav-aged and the beaver destroyed in what must have been a violent encounter with something so ferocious and with an appetite for the death of its victims. Father would never believe that an animal could be killed so mercilessly. The beautiful beaver fur had been torn to shreds by sharp razor-like claws and left in tatters. No way could the pelt be saved, but the meat could still be used to feed his hungry family. Disgusted, Erick threw it onto his sled along with his trap.

Unhappy but still feeling confident about his next trap containing a prize beaver, Erick moved forward along Potato Creek. He knew his third trap was getting close and then he saw his marker stake. This time he approached the stake with caution and noticed indications of something underneath the snow. Right at the stake was a mound of what he knew must be his frozen beaver. He began to dig the snow away. Excitement and exhilaration rushed through Erick's body as fur came into view, but the excitement was short lived as he saw the fur was completely encrusted with the beaver's blood. Once again Erick's hopes were dashed to pieces as he looked at yet another beautiful animal, mauled, torn, and shredded to a point that the beaver could not be recognized. Again he threw the carcass onto his sled, now loathing whatever it was in these woods that was killing these beavers. It was apparent that whatever was doing the killing was not doing it to eat. Its only apparent intention was to mercilessly kill.

Erick could list only one killer that could do such a thing. These poor animals were dismembered and disemboweled. That fact pointed the finger of guilt to only one thing. Erick picked up his rifle, making sure he had a bullet in the chamber, and walked on. In addition to collecting his traps, he knew he now also had to concentrate on protecting himself. Erick walked slower and slower and spent more time looking at the woods to his right and to the creek down below.

He found his next trap without any difficulty. A thin coat of ice covered his original chopped hole but he cut it out in moments and saw fur just below the water. Erick started to panic as blood rose up into the chopped hole. He removed his mittens that Mother had made him from fox skins the year before. Erick's deliberate slowness was caused by the realization that down in that hole was, once again, another despicable act of mutilation. He finally came up with the courage to reach down and pull up the chain holding the trap and its victim. Again it was a beaver and again it had fallen victim to some traumatic assault.

The beaver came out of the water torn to shreds with blood soaked fur. Erick was now confused by the fact that these beavers had been deliberately and viciously destroyed. These acts brought to mind the Namekagan men, which he feared from his father's stories. He remembered from the stories that they had killed viciously, but they had eaten their victims. Whatever this was, it couldn't be the Namekagan men for that reason alone. Once again, the beaver fur would be worthless but the meat could still be saved since it had been preserved down in that cold clear water since it was killed.

Erick put another destroyed beaver onto his sled and headed out to his next trap. Erick had always had a happy-go-lucky personality. But now, his sense of humor was long gone since finding the first mutilated beaver. He used to whistle and hum as he did his chores at home. But since finding the beavers so mutilated, his attitude was replaced by unhappiness and discouragement. He decided to go on, so he towed his sleds with the damaged pelts and retrieved traps and stakes. On down the trap line he traveled.

Ahead, he saw one of his fox traps partially swinging from some low brush. As he approached, he could see the trap was empty and that it had been set off. There was no fox. *Well, certainly no surprise there,* he thought, *surely no one on earth can be this unlucky.* He picked up his trap and threw it violently toward the sled, missed, and bent down to retrieve the trap, then placed it on his sled.

Erick moved along the creek's embankment toward his next trap. A second fox trap was in sight and, as he approached, he could see it was empty and had been set off. Blood and fur chunks were scattered everywhere, sticking up through the snow cover. Possibly the fox had eaten off his leg to get free from the trap, or could it be something else? Erick hadn't walked but a couple of yards when he saw a leg protruding through the snow. Undoubtedly from the fur color, it had been a red fox. As he looked for evidence of what had happened at his trap, he came across the site of the fox's final struggle for life that had only ended in one more vicious killing. The fox's life had been snuffed out here on this very spot.

There was no sense trying to salvage any meat and it was hopeless to even think of taking the fur. Erick knew all that was left was a snack for either the eagles or wolves, depending on which ones arrived first. He placed his trap onto the sled and moved on along the creek.

A doe and her yearling suddenly appeared in front of him. Erick made quick eye contact with the doe and she threw up her white warning flag and bounded off toward the darkened woods, closely followed by her tiny young one.

An eagle flew in low, threatening circles overhead, screeching its displeasure with Erick being in its woods. Erick could almost hear him say, "Move on, little boy, so I can come down and snack."

Onward Erick trekked, dragging his sleds behind him. He found his next two beaver traps in much the same way as his previous ones—with over fifty pounds of unrecognizable beaver in each. He reached down to pull up the first beaver only to discover it was mutilated even worse than the others. The second one was torn to shreds leaving him with another worthless pelt. Erick threw his two beavers onto the sled, disgusted beyond words. Wild thoughts started running rampant through his mind that perhaps the Namekagan men were following him deep into the Lotorp wilderness and were ruining his traps.

Snow continued to fall as it had done for nearly two days. Erick thought of his little camp and his huge stack of dry firewood. Luckily, he'd had the forethought to cut, chop, and stack his wood safely under the shelter of the pine boughs. Erick also gave continuing thought to his father and mother. He knew they were most likely waiting at the cabin window, worrying and fretting. He also thought of his warm comfortable bed in the corner of the room. Never, never again would he complain that the bed leaned down toward the wall and that the ropes tied together holding up his blankets were broken. So what if the blankets dragged on the wooden planked floor. No more complaining and no more whining that some of the ropes were missing. Erick knew now that there were more important things in life than frivolous details.

Oh, what he would give to be sitting in front of the family fireplace, smelling the continuous cooking and baking. He could smell the chicken fat bubbling to the surface of Mother's soon-to-be chicken soup. He could see Mother *in winter?*

peeling, cutting, and gently lowering the fresh vegetables into the boiling chicken broth to make it into soup. The sweet smells of fresh baked breads of all kinds filled his mind, as well as her varieties of fabulous fresh cookies. Spring brought rhubarb and summer brought strawberry rhubarb or cloudberry pies that Mother would put out on the window ledge to cool. More than once, Father had been caught sneaking beneath the window and taking a sample or two, but he was usually caught red-handed and punished severely for his childish behavior.

Throughout the summer, Mother would cut fresh flowers from her garden and bring them into the cabin, adding the sweet smells of flowers to the dank cabin home. The cabin was set on one hundred and sixty acres of woods and four acres of cultivated fields. The cabin was a constant in Erick's family life. It was the backdrop for an untold number of Sundays, holidays, games, and birthday parties, as well as sad occasions like funeral gatherings.

Mother had a window between the fireplace and big featherbed which she always looked out. When weather permitted, little Charles would play on the teeter-totter Father had built directly in front of Mother's window. Other than the teeter-totter, there wasn't much else to do except the chores you were assigned. The most important chores in the family were always assigned to Erick. His chore was to carry out the garbage, far out to the edge of the woods. His tool was the sharpened spade. Mother would always say, "Now Erick, you be sure to bury everything deep so that the bears can't smell the garbage and follow the aroma in to dig it up." Thinking of the aroma of the garbage, Erick shuddered remembering his Mother's ground fish soup, which he found disturbingly distasteful.

Erick pictured his Grandfather Ernst, Grandmother Anna, Father, Mother, and little Charles all gathered around the family fireplace, all as snug as a bug in a rug on a wintry day. Each and every one would be begging Father to tell one of his stories. Erick thought of his father sipping hot porridge and of the porridge hanging down from his mustache like it always did. This was always followed by Mother giving Father a severe scolding, but with a broad smile. Erick took comfort in the fact that there were people in the world that cared about him and loved him.

Knowing that someone or something was preventing him from bringing home a sled load of meat and prime pelts kept Erick's spirits down. What would they think back at the little schoolhouse Erick attended? It was December, the middle of winter, and classes had been canceled because of the heavy snow. When classes started up again, his story would surely race through school like a prairie fire. How long would it take in a one-room school? How could he ever show himself in Lotorp again? Now when he would go into the mercantile for his piece of licorice, everyone's eyes would fall on him, fingers would point to him, and town laughter would all be directed at him.

As it was, Erick stood out in town like a bull moose at a church gathering. He wore a loose-fitting blanket type of coat made from wool. Mother had dyed it bright red with three black stripes around one sleeve. She added the stripes because that was the way Swedish trappers and hunters determined the prices of blankets and clothing. Each stripe was equivalent to one beaver pelt in trade at the mercantile. So, when she dyed on the three stripes, it meant that Mother thought the coat had the value of three beaver pelts. A woolen blanket with eight stripes would cost eight beaver pelts and this was how costs were determined. Everything was simple and no money had to change hands. Erick's blanket coat was a long heavy garment that hung down almost to his furry, knee-high, mooseskin boots. His coat was held closed with buttons made from small spike deer antlers. He wore a furry coyote hat with a long bushy tail that hung halfway down his back. His birch bark leggings were a sure giveaway to the fact that he was from the wilderness and not town. In addition, he always carried his rifle wherever he went. Neighboring farm children would always poke fun at Erick for wearing his birch bark leggings to school during the winter months. Erick's failure to bring home the prime beaver pelts after over a week out in the Lotorp wilderness would surely bring shame and dishonor to the Holm family. Grandfather and Grandmother could possibly lose the respect of the whole community.

Erick reasoned that his mopish behavior was not going to fill his last nine traps. He moved on again along Potato Creek. The next trap was just ahead. He let the sled rope loose and hiked down what was now a steep embankment to the creek. His steel stake protruded up through the ice and snow. He chopped a fresh hole in the existing ice hole, lifted the four feet of chain connecting the stake to the trap. The trap felt light and his heart sank as his empty trap bubbled to the creek's surface.

Erick simply stood there staring down at the empty trap, which he noticed had been triggered and had clamped closed on itself. The intestines that had been used for bait had also been eaten. Erick prided himself on reading people and animals, but some animals can fool you. He figured he shouldn't fret too long about his predicament or it would drive him mad. "I guess evil holds no preference for its victim. Nothing in the trap again," he screamed out loud, feeling pity for himself. Once again tears rolled down his frozen little cheeks. They froze before reaching his chin. The tears had cleared thin pathways down his dirty little face. He tried wiping the tears away with his coat but only succeeded in making a big dirty mess. His face was completely filthy except for the clean lines left by his tears.

He snapped out of his self-pity when he looked down and noticed deep tracks in the falling snow. He was not alone. One, two, three, four, five toes he counted, and a large pad behind. This was the evidence Erick had waited long and hard for. Here was indisputable evidence as to the killer of his beavers and fox and evidence that he had been watched and followed by the most notorious and vicious killer in all the North Woods. This treacherous animal was the most elusive of all the animals in the woods and was known to kill for the sake of killing. Now Erick knew what his adversary was. He grew cold and sweat started beading up on his dirty, crusted brow. "Badger," Erick said out loud. With that, he hurried along picking up his trap and climbing back up the embankment.

Directly ahead stood a tall stand of jack pine he remembered going around when he had set the traps. This time, everything seemed a little sinister and scary. He knew he couldn't walk on the creek to get around and the pines were too dense to cut through so he had to walk around the pines. Badger or no badger, he was going to pick up the rest of his trap line. He pulled his rifle from its protective sheath of elk skin and pulled back the bolt, just to reassure himself that the bullet was safely in the chamber. He snapped it closed and placed the sling over his right shoulder. He unsnapped his jacket pocket buttons holding additional bullets and made sure that they were at the ready in case they were needed.

Erick knew very little about badgers, but his father's stories brought a chill through his body. Each time one of his father's stories had a badger in it, the story always ended horribly, and Father would end the story by saying that they were killing machines.

Erick inched closer to the jack pines with his eyes closely glued to the darkness within them. He was relieved when he came around the far edge of the pines and saw the creek once again. *No more tracks,* he thought as he pulled his sleds forward.

Again he left his sleds when he saw the next shiny steel stake sitting up out of the creek ice. He looked the area over carefully before kneeling down in the deep snow to chop out the trap. He lowered his rifle and leaned it up against a white birch that was leaning over the creek's edge. He chopped fast and furious to get down to the chain links. His mouth was so very dry that he cupped his hands together for a cold drink of creek water. It tasted wonderful. He looked down into the cold clear water thinking of the natural springs that must have kept this water so clean for hundreds, maybe thousands of years. With that, he reached down and pulled on the chain. "Oh, thank God," he sighed as he felt a weight at the other end. He pulled up his trap slowly but he realized he had another beaver that was torn and tattered. Again he felt bad for the poor helpless creature that God had created and that the badger had torn the life from. He looked again in disbelief at the creature half eaten into pieces and the rest mauled. It looked like a pack of wolves had attacked the poor defenseless trapped animal, trapped in Erick's trap.

He unclamped the beaver from the trap and placed both the trap and beaver on the sled. He slung his rifle onto his shoulder and moved on along the creek. He stared blankly ahead thinking nothing in the world could possibly be as bad as his current situation. Snow and sleet were pelting him in his face with every step. He knew his final traps lay within the next mile. He thought long and hard whether he should go on or just give up, return home, and live the life of a monk in some far away monastery until he became old and gray.

Erick didn't have to think long; he was not a quitter, nor was his family. He was not about to start quitting now.

The snow came down heavier and faster. Erick held fast, listening intently. He heard a call that he knew well; it was a bull moose calling a cow moose for a rendezvous. The bull gave his sexiest love call, which gradually increased in tone until high-pitched sounds echoed over the snow-covered forest. Erick translated the love song to mean, "Let's meet for a little courtship." The loud sounds slowly subsided to loving, pleasing sounds that Erick had heard dozens of times in the forest with his father. Cow moose, if they were interested, usually returned such calls between nightfall and the early morning. Those calls would start as very high-pitched sounds and would slowly increase in volume as they continued.

Erick was motionless and excited over the moose courtship taking place right there near him. Father had said the bull would roam all through the woods and marshes listening for the love song of the cows that would usually submit to the love calls. Father had told Erick that while the bull moose was seeking marriage, the cow would sing her love song. Just then Erick heard the cow's love song again coming from behind the heavy falling snow. The bull answered with a trampling of underbrush and a slashing of antlers against the brush and soft pine trees. Erick was trembling as he heard a hollow crashing. Erick remembered Father saying that right before the cow and bull would marry, the bull would dig out a shallow trough in the snow or earth with his hoofs. The bull would then irrigate the trough by urinating into it. This would be followed by the bull trampling the area with his hoofs and rolling in the urine and snow or dirt mix. A cow could detect the resulting stench for miles. Erick decided that he was in the center of what could be conceived as a love triangle, which he knew could be as dangerous as a badger pursuing him. Erick decided to put some distance between him and the consummation of the moose marriage. Erick changed directions and made a wide turn around the moose couple.

By now, Erick looked like a snowman. The large snowflakes clung to him and turned him a solid white. The snow covered him completely and made him look like a small tree stump sticking out of the crust of packed snow. He could barely see the creek edge, but he plodded forward. The wet snow clung to everything it touched and kept falling. The creek and forest seemed to be one now. Snow clung to the trees. Only days before, the pine branches had reached toward the sky. They now bowed to the heavy weight of snow as their shoulders bent toward the ground.

CHAPTER FIVE

Erick could hardly see two feet in front of him. He was getting a little bit frightened as he realized the snowstorm had turned into a full-blown blizzard. Judging from the big soft flakes, he knew the temperature was getting warmer but he also knew that a deep cold always followed the day or night after a snowstorm. He pushed on through the blizzard, finally coming upon his last trap, half buried under the deep, fresh snow. Quickly chopping through the thin ice that had formed since he set the trap, he began pulling up the chain. He felt weight at the other end. "Oh please, Lord, let it be undamaged," he prayed. Up came the beaver, breaking the surface of the creek, so badly damaged that only he could identify this mound of fur as a once living animal. Only the meat could be saved.

He tied the beaver and his last trap onto the snow-covered sled and turned the sled completely around, Erick was heading back to camp. He gave very little thought to all the dangers he had faced on his trip. His only thoughts were on not coming home with two sled loads of meat and prime beaver pelts. Sadder still, the only mink he had seen on his whole trip was one he had seen chasing a frog down one of his chopped ice holes. Was it so wrong to expect a sled load or two of prime beaver pelts? Was it so ridiculous to expect possibly a half dozen silver fox pelts to adorn his sled? As Erick's mind skipped along, the heavy snow continued to fall. It became harder and harder for him to pull the heavy sled. His campsite was still another two miles ahead along the creek. *One thing is for sure,* he thought, *even in the snow, I can't get lost by following the creek.* He kept a constant eye on the creek as it wound along through the forest. It gave Erick comfort knowing his camp was just ahead.

Just then, something caught Erick's attention. His eyes picked up a slight movement out toward the forest's edge. It was a lone wolf. Erick stood quietly and watched the wolf with respect and caution. The wolf seemed nervous and with every few steps he would stop and look around. It became more obvious that the wolf was more concerned with what was behind him than what might be in front of him. This was more than just curious to Erick; it was downright intimidating. The wolf was not especially large—only about seventy-five pounds—and it was a filthy gray color with thick hair matted down from the blood of many sumptuous meals. The nervous wolf walked slowly toward Erick. It walked a few steps closer and again turned around, as if expecting something to appear out of the forest's edge. It stood there and just waited again, looking over his shoulder at the darkened woods. Then it turned toward Erick. Erick could see directly into its eyes. They were not cold and yellow like a typical wolf, but warm and brown. Even from twenty-five yards, Erick could see the fear and worry in the wolf's soft brown eyes.

Erick had just skinned out three beavers and had hung them up from a birch tree. The smell of the dressed beavers must have attracted the wolf, but the wolf seemed to cower and tremble. Erick's rifle was loaded and ready. The smooth oak butt of his rifle fit easily against his shoulder. Erick waited, knowing something had frightened this wolf half to death. The trembling wolf began to whine but stayed put at twenty-five yards, as if frozen in place. Erick removed the safety from the rifle and slowly pressed his finger to the trigger. A giant beast of a wolf, black as night, came crashing out of the woods and exploded toward Erick at top speed. He flew past the trembling smaller wolf that was so scared he wet himself, turning the fresh snow yellow. Erick's rifle exploded just in time, causing the big black beast to lay motionless at Erick's boot. It was the biggest wolf that Erick had ever seen or even heard of.

Erick looked down as the beast's tongue slowly slid out of his foaming mouth. *No wonder the other wolf was in fear for its life. The big beast had rabies,* Erick thought. He looked up away from the rabid wolf as its pack slowly circled the little clearing. Erick reloaded and aimed at the closest wolf in the pack. The shot was like a clap of thunder as the sound resonated through the forest. The pack scattered as Erick quickly reloaded. There was no time to aim as Erick fired from his hip at a trailing wolf that raced toward him. The forest solitude was shattered by the third rifle shot. The deafening sound rumbled through the forest as a second wolf dropped to the snow dead.

Erick noticed that his body was shaking and trembling as he bent down to examine has trophy-sized wolves. Erick had himself two beautiful pelts, which made up at least a little for his disastrous trapping trip. These pelts would fetch a tidy amount at the Lotorp market on Saturday, he was sure. As for the wolfpack, they would have to find themselves another bold and fearless leader, because their leader had met someone superior and then some. Erick smiled to himself, *Not so bad. Three bullets and two wolves. Father will be thrilled. Mother and little Charles will cry.* Erick would now be Big Brother the Wolf Killer to little Charles.

The snow was so deep that Erick had to put on his snow-shoes. They slowed him down, but they kept him dry. He pulled his sled through the deepening drifts. With each step, he was thankful for his birch bark leggings. If not for those and his snowshoes, he would not have been able to go another step. Once again, Erick thought of his little bed in the corner of the cabin. He had neglected to repair his bed ropes before his trapping trip. The left bottom corner of the bed hung down to the floor because the ropes that held the woolen blankets had unraveled and become loose. He meant to replace the ropes but had never gotten around to the task. *After all,* he had thought, *I can replace the ropes anytime except trapping season.* He was determined to think no more about home; he had to concentrate on survival.

He came across fresh deer tracks and he could tell they had to be from a good size buck or a doe with her unborn fawn that she was ready to drop in the snow. It was, after all, almost the time of year for birthing. Erick rounded a bend in the creek and felt a sudden stiff wind and blowing snow. He tried walking backward but he gave that up after falling several times and deciding it was stupid and foolish, not to mention dangerous. He still had another half mile to go. His long blond hair was wringing wet and hung like strands of seaweed. He looked ahead but saw no sign of his camp. Looking down on his sled load of traps, damaged skins, and beaver meat, he came to realize that his whole trip had been a nightmarish mistake.

He saw that there was an overhang up ahead that would afford him protection from the snow, which had now slowed down and had turned into smaller flakes. He pulled his sled up close and examined the overhang. It was similar to a cave that went in about ten yards. *What a great place for a bear den,* he thought. He checked it out completely just to make sure no bear had been there or would be returning. He cut some kindling and started a fire. It didn't take long before Erick had a rip-roaring fire blazing. He pulled his sled under the overhang and sat down. He looked out and decided that he would stay here for the night rather than walk any further.

Erick knew the proverb, "You made your bed, now lie in it." He knew it was usually said by self-righteously smug types to their less fortunate brethren who had gotten themselves into a mess and couldn't get out of it. Poor Erick felt he fit that description perfectly. Close by, an owl hooted and Erick knew that small animals would be running for cover.

Erick had walked a great distance since his close encounter with the love song of the moose. Just then the distant loud bellowing of the bull broke the night air. Erick felt that death and danger were keeping a steady pace with him on his travels. Tonight, without a hunter's moon and with the snow falling slowly, Erick sensed there would be death in the Lotorp woods.

As wildly remote and beautiful as the Lotorp wilderness was, it held Erick captive under the overhang. His common sense about weather conditions dictated his decision to stay put. Erick looked out at miles of white, sparkling snow. As he sat in front of the fire, he thought of his father's teachings. Erick's mind was like a cloud of gnats, always in constant motion and unable to completely rest. Father had spent a lot of time on the extremely important details of sighting in Erick's rifle, so that his bullet would hit exactly where Erick would aim it. Father taught Erick that the sights could only be adjusted on a cold rifle. Then he could only fire three times. Then he'd have to wait for the rifle to get cool again before testing his sights on the target. Father said that the rifle might shoot to an entirely different spot when the rifle got hot from firing. "In hunting," he would say, "you will only have one chance and that chance could save your life when faced with a dangerous animal." He went on to tell Erick that the biggest factor in getting a bullet into a vital zone depended more on the shooter than the weapon itself.

Erick was up late and unable to sleep. He had too much on his mind to relax. He worried that dawn would be breaking through the eastern sky soon. He hoped the morning sun would bring him a pleasant day for a change.

CHAPTER SIX

Erick broke off a piece of Mother's bread. After finishing the bread, he opened his coat and removed Father's skinning knife from its sheath on his hip. The knife handle was as long as the blade and was made from a long section of moose antler. Father had fashioned the handle to his liking years before Erick was born. Erick then took out his sharpening stone and sat quietly for a moment. He held the knife in front of him and stared, momentarily mesmerized by the brightly shining metal blade. He then spit on the stone and began to sharpen one edge at a time. Erick had all the time in the world to sharpen Father's knife. He wanted it honed to perfection for the skinning he knew would be necessary. Father had told him that every good woodsman knew to pay attention while sharpening a blade. If you didn't pay attention, sooner or later, out in the woods alone, you would bleed to death and the varmints would pick your bones clean.

Erick's stomach was growling loudly, so loud in fact, that he began to worry that a coyote or wolf might hear. He finished sharpening the knife and wiped the glistening blade on the leg of his pants. The knife was perfectly balanced and fit in the palm of his hand as if he had been born with the knife there. Erick thought about the next morning and how he had no food left except the mutilated beavers. Possibly to survive, he would have to sacrifice some of his principles for the sake of food. Father always said to never kill an animal unless you planned on having it to eat. If he shot a deer or elk to satisfy his hunger, surely the rest would not go to waste.

Erick could feel his ribs protruding through his tightened skin and knew he had to get something to eat and quick. Pulling those sleds loaded with beaver had depleted his energy. He made up his mind; he would hunt for food come daylight. Erick had passed a well-used game trail awhile back. The trail wound along a perimeter of a wide oval-shaped tamarack swamp set deep in a hollow between two steep ridges. It was ideal for bedded down deer or elk. This is where Erick had passed deer before. He also had to keep in mind that any tamarack swamp was the natural habitat to the black and grizzly bear. He had no dog to protect him as an early warning system. Dogs could smell a grizzly for a half a mile or so.

Erick sat by the campfire and began to oil his rifle. He cleaned the muzzle and breach with his light gun oil and cloth. He took additional bullets from his pouch and tucked them safely away in his jacket pocket. He went over to a sled and cut a beaver down the middle, removed a gut section, and wrapped the guts in one of Mother's bait bags. He was now ready for the hunt in the morning.

Dawn came cold and crisp. Erick rekindled his fire, drank some warmed coffee, and was off, taking his gut bag and skinned out beaver. He tied the beaver pelt onto a rope and the rope around his thigh. In this way, his hands were not occupied except for his rifle. He deliberately dragged the beaver pelt behind him to cover his own scent. He moved along the game trail for at least two miles dragging the pelt behind. He saw no signs of any tracks in those miles. He was laying down an irresistible scent trail of a wounded beaver. No deer or elk could pick up on Erick's scent with the strong beaver scent covering Erick's. Father had taught Erick a little trick that involved apples and manure. When Father would hunt for deer or elk, he would cut up apples and smear the apple juices all over his exposed skin and as much on his clothing as possible. Then Father would go out to the barn and smear fresh cow manure over his jacket and pants. The combination of apple juice and manure always worked, as Father always came home with a trophy buck. The animals that Father hunted could not detect his human scent and therefore never suspected any danger approaching. Father would always say that not one white flag ever came up in a herd of deer due to his proven scent killer.

Erick had no apples or manure, so he used what he did have: beaver pelts. Erick walked another mile but worried that the deer or elk would hear the loud growling of his stomach. He thought of his mother at her open fireplace cooking. He imagined the smell of fresh liver and onions. He reminisced on the pungent odors coming from her pan.

Erick climbed to the top of a ridge where he could overlook the valley. If Erick had looked up or behind him, he would have noticed an assemblage of bluejays circling, and gray and black squirrels following his beaver pelt. Erick finally stopped and looked up at the bluejays creating a scene with their loud squawking. Then came a pair of northern goshawks, the gray ghost rapiers. They were gray like the color of gun smoke and had eyes that glowed like live embers. Their wings were silent and their gripping feet were tipped with daggers. Alarms were triggered from the other birds as a great gray owl swooped low waiting for a free dinner from Erick's beaver pelt. These were all the foragers of the forest. Erick felt he should have just tied a loud dinner bell around his neck. These birds were making so much noise it must have caught the attention of every animal in the swamp and beyond. Erick, having the same wonderful sense of humor as his father, began to laugh at his own joke.

His laughter was short lived however, as across the tamarack swamp appeared the silhouette of a fully-grown black bear. Erick was about to find his hands full of something he did not want or need. He was, after all, only looking for a buck to quiet his growling stomach.

Erick watched intently as the black bear ambled across the swamp and deep snow. Closer and closer he came. Erick wondered what awoke this giant from its winter hibernation. The bluejays, northern goshawks, and great gray owl scattered for protective cover. The big bear stopped every few seconds to test the clear air with its sensitive nose, waving its head back and forth like a flag, searching for scents he could identify. Erick, being only seven, didn't have enough experience to know if the bear was a male or female, but as the bear got closer, its sex seemed insignificant. The beast was mammoth and black as freshly mined coal.

Erick's heart began to pound nearly out of his chest. Now, he had all the makings of a nightmare. He could hear his extra bullets clinking against each other in his jacket pocket. Perspiration ran down Erick's face and the small of his back. His face turned bright white as all the color drained from his cheeks. He gripped his rifle tighter and tighter. His knuckles turned snow white as he applied more pressure to the rifle. The bear just kept coming and was now about fifty yards from Erick. Erick took off his right mitten, placed it in front of him, and laid two additional bullets in it.

The bear hesitated briefly, but then began to pound the snow pack with its front paw. It huffed and huffed and huffed. It sounded to Erick as if the bear was definitely mad about something, possibly Erick being in the woods. Quite visible now were its feet, tipped with long black claws that turned down for better gouging and tearing of its victims.

Grandfather and Father had both told stories as far back as he could remember. The story that flashed in Erick's mind was of the blueberry picker and the black bear. The blueberry picker was an old man, maybe forty, alone picking berries in a thick and deep berry patch. He was concentrating on filling his three wooden buckets with the big succulent blue delights. He was backing up slowly, placing berries in his buckets and eating them at the same time. He would stand on his tiptoes to reach the bigger berries, deep within the bushes. He suddenly felt pain across the back of both of his legs. Dropping his bucket, the berries flew in every direction. The man looked down and saw four long, deep crimson slashes across both of his legs. Blood began spurting out from all four openings. The man pivoted his body around as a big black silhouette covered him. There was a black bear staring straight down into the picker's eyes. They were eyeball to eyeball and neither one flexed a muscle. The bear took another swing with his giant paw, raking four more deep cuts across the picker's chest. Now blood was spurting endlessly from the man's wounds. Both the berry picker and the bear stood six feet tall.

The bear raised his paw and swung violently again, but he missed and cut harmlessly through the blueberry bushes. Berry branches and berries flew everywhere with berry juices covering the picker as well as the bear. The picker fainted dead away as the bear's paw missed him. He lay motionless in a crumpled heap with blood gushing from his wounds. The bear pawed his victim a few times and then bit and tore away mounds of flesh and muscle from its berry-picking partner. The bear stared down at his victim and then went back to his own berry picking. After taking care of the intruder in his berry patch, he got right back into the rhythm of picking berries.

It had been a fateful day for the old man. He had been unlucky enough to choose to pick berries from the same patch as the black bear. The bear continued his picking and eating as the old berry picker lay stone dead at his feet.

Erick flashed back to the reality of the moment, trying to put the story out of his mind and how the bear's claws had killed the picker in only seconds. The bear just kept moving closer to Erick. Its claws were more than four inches long and seemed to glisten in the light. Erick wanted no part of this black bear and kept praying the monster would turn away and become attracted to something other than him. The bear suddenly became agitated, stood up on its back legs, and began moving its neck from side to side, snapping its jaws and swinging its front paws wildly in the air. Then it dropped down onto all four feet again. It violently pounded the snow pack as if it had a fire in its belly and was trying to put it out. Erick wished he were back home in his little bed against the wall in the corner of the room. Erick lay down in the snow, prone, pulling his hand tightly into the sling to steady his rifle, digging his elbows deep into the snow to steady it. He placed his oak rifle butt up against his right shoulder. Trembling and shaking, Erick's body gave a violent shiver and he took a long deep breath as the black bear grew louder and closer. The bear's growling seemed to come from a fire deep within its soul, if indeed it had one.

Erick totally concentrated, as if in a trance, remembering how his grandfather and father had trained him. "First and foremost," they had said, "never shoot early, and secondly, always squeeze the trigger as if in slow motion."

This massive bundle of dark black muscle and meanness now came through the tamarack huffing and huffing like a

steam freight train coming up a steep mountain grade. The bear was so close now that Erick could see the hot breath coming out of the beast's nostrils and fire raging in its eyes as it hit its full stride. Lying prone in the snow, Erick could feel each oncoming step of the giant vibrating through his body. A northern goshawk caught Erick's eye as it swooped down low as if to get a better view of the upcoming action. The bear's small dark black eyes were wet and glassed over as if its black heart was going to explode with contempt and anger at this intruder of its forest domain. The bear was now twenty yards from Erick and closing the distance fast. The bear had Erick's scent now and was coming in for the kill. Erick began to squeeze the trigger, like Father had taught him hundreds of times before. The sound of the rifle was deafening and its force pushed Erick backward in the snow. Smoke from the gunpowder circled above Erick's head like a halo.

The fifty-caliber bullet found its mark. The bullet went through the black bear's little black eye and out through its brain, but the beast just kept coming, blood spurting in every direction onto the clean, white snow, now rapidly turning the color of a cranberry marsh. As the black bear continued running toward Erick, its body folded like a giant black circus tent.

Erick's rifle was knocked out of his hands and propelled like a stone deep into the snow, not by the black bear Erick had shot, but by a second black bear. Erick was crushed down deep into the snow from the bear's weight as it came to its final resting place. Erick's face was buried deep in the snow. The second black bear covered him completely. He turned his neck and looked up. He could see the bear that he had shot lying dead only three yards away. Erick had killed it instantly with the shot to the brain, but it took a few more yards until the dead bear actually folded down under its own weight. The second bear was not moving as it lay on top of Erick. Saliva was drooling down onto Erick's face from the second bear's open mouth. The second bear's one remaining black eye stared down at Erick. The bear's open mouth could have engulfed Erick's whole head if it had been given the chance. He could smell the bear's rotten breath coming out of his now dead lungs. The bear's open mouth and long white teeth were just inches away from Erick's ear. The second bear turned out to be identical to the first. Erick was pressed down under the bear's weight like a hammer on a nail. He slowly dug his way out. He pushed the enormous brute slowly with all his might and managed to wiggle free. Miraculously, he hadn't broken anything, and, as far as he could tell, none of the blood on him was his.

The bear's gaping, bloody mouth was still wide open. It had died during his last futile attempt to devour the prey it was attacking, which just happened to be Erick. Its claws looked as long as Erick's head and could have decapitated him in one swipe. Erick stood up shakily, looked down at the second bear, now with its long leathery pink tongue drooling into the crimson snow. A cold chill ran through Erick's body as he realized this second bear had also been shot through the eye and that the bullet had lodged in its brain. Erick stood mystified, bewildered, and in total disbelief that he had killed two black bears with one single bullet. These two bears must have been twin sisters, eating, playing, living, and hunting together since birth. Never separated, not even in death.

CHAPTER SEVEN

All this flashed through Erick's mind as he tried to relive this puzzling, unbelievable spectacle. He hurriedly looked around this now despicable death scene for his rifle. Finding its barrel partially exposed beneath the second bear's rump, he pulled the rifle out from under the bear only to find the solid oak stock had broken off and was completely missing. He tried to reload the remains of his once precious Christmas present from Grandfather Ernst. He dropped bullet after bullet with his cold trembling fingers. Wild thoughts of the possibility of a third bear watching and waiting raced through his mind. Could there be another waiting for an opportunity to finish what its two sisters had failed to accomplish?

"Erick! Erick!" called a voice. Erick wondered if he had gone mad or been killed and perhaps he was hearing the voice of God calling him to come join his ancestors. Again the voice called, "Erick! Erick!" He looked behind him in the direction of the voice. Up on the ridgeline, he caught sight of a lone figure coming down on snowshoes. He was astonished to see his Grandfather Ernst.

Grandfather was cautiously making his way down the ridgeline. As Grandfather grew closer, Erick could see his fifty-caliber rifle slung over his shoulder. Erick began to yell, "Grandfather, Grandfather! It was you that killed the second bear, wasn't it?" Now Erick began to tremble and cry uncontrollably.

Grandfather had finally reached Erick. Grandfather's ruddy complexion seemed to set off and highlight his beet-red face brought about by his rapid trip down on snowshoes. Grandfather threw his arms around Erick. He hugged the boy tightly to his massive chest and lifted him high over his head into the air while crying himself.

"Please don't cry, Grandfather, please stop."

"I can't stop, Erick, I just can't stop. I almost lost you to the second bear. I know you never saw the second bear coming up behind you, did you?"

"No, Grandfather, I didn't see him or hear him. I was concentrating so hard on the bear running straight at me that nothing else entered my mind. You saved my life, Grandfather."

"That's going to be our little secret. Your mother and father can be spared the frightening details. We are not going to tell them about the second bear sneaking up behind you."

"Grandfather, what are you doing out here?"

"Your mother and father have been terrified that something may have happened to you. They were desperately worried about you and your mother pleaded with me to go out and find you, to bring you home. Your mother has cried her eyes out every day since you left. Don't say anything, but your father cries, too."

"How did you ever find me way out here?"

"You were so easy to find. I just followed Potato Creek, like you did."

"I have so much to tell you—" Erick started to say.

"That can wait, Erick," Grandfather interrupted. "Let's get these two mammoths strung up first. Oh, by the way, I brought you a little present." Grandfather removed his knap-sack from his back and leaned his rifle next to it. He bent down and opened the side flap wide so Erick could watch. "Let's see," he said, "I am sure I remembered to bring it with me. Oh, there it is." And with that Grandfather pulled out two pieces of licorice.

Erick's smile could have lit up a room. "Thank you, Grandfather," he said with tears rolling down his little face.

"Well, Erick, you start telling me all about your trapping adventures while I gut and clean this first bruiser."

Erick told Grandfather each and every detail of his adventures. Grandfather finished gutting the first of the bear sisters and then the two of them strung up the second sister. It was getting dark as Grandfather finished gutting the sec-ond sister.

"Let's get back to your camp, Erick. I passed it not too far back along the creek. I dropped off my sled at your camp. I hope you don't mind a little bit of company tonight," he joked. "I promised your mother that when I did find you, I would bring you straight home, so that's what we will do tomorrow. We can come back in the morning for one bear and load it onto my sled. I can come back in a few days for the second bear. It will be fine, hanging up there until then."

Erick asked, "Will my parents let me come back with you to pick up the second bear?"

"I am sure they will. I'll put in a good word for you. I will swear up and down that you were never in any danger," he said with a chuckle. "I will lie my face off and tell enor-mous fibs until I am tied in knots for you, Erick. Your moth-er must never know. Now, cross your heart and hope to die." Erick did so.

"Not telling your mother will not make us loathed and despicable sinners. The gates of heaven won't roll closed in our faces as our ancestors look on. You look a little pale, Erick. Don't worry, you will not spend eternity in the fires of hell. Stop trembling; it's just that we're not telling your mother the rest of the story about the twin black bear sisters. I won't suffer from hemorrhoids all the rest of my life due to a little white fib."

Erick simply stared at Grandfather, not knowing what a hemorrhoid was and afraid to ask if it was something one ate.

"Let's both pray that your mother's in a lighthearted mood when get back, for our sake. What's done is done and you're not hurt or injured. I'll tell you what, Erick. We will tell your children the whole story together in twenty-five years, how about that?"

"That sounds fine, Grandfather, twenty-five years, that's a deal."

CHAPTER EIGHT

Erick and Grandfather awoke early, before dawn, due entirely to their fire going out. They awoke to a winter wonderland of fresh bright snow that was still falling. Grandfather jokingly asked Erick if he thought the snow was deep enough for snow skis and, with a hearty laugh, he strapped his on. Somehow, the two of them had to escape from the obliterating and frigid blizzard. The two looked like a pair of Birkebeiner skiers, so called for the protective birch bark leggings they wore. Birkebeiner, or Birkalar, were Swedish trappers who explored and colonized. Swedish kings gave them permission to exploit their wilderness, amassing furs and fish. These frontiersmen took bark from birch trees and made leggings to protect them while skiing.

The severe weather meant it wouldn't be so easy to drag the black bear behind them. Erick thought back to the previous day when he first noticed the wind shift out of the north. He noticed that the air had become cold and raw. The wind had always been at his back until that shift.

They only had a mile to go before they would have a crackling fire blazing under the lean-to of boughs that Erick had put together. By now, the boughs should be a solid block of ice and snow that would protect them from the cold blizzard conditions.

The wind was unrelenting as they skied through the heavy packed snow. They tried to hurry their slow progress but gave up after only a few yards due to the snow skis awkwardness in pulling the sleds. Their sight became limited to only a yard or two. Erick figured his lean-to of boughs must be just ahead, but where? Erick screamed into the biting wind, "Please, Lord help." His words only blew back in his face without answer.

Erick's woolen jacket was soaking wet but he was dry under the heavy wool. Erick and Grandfather both had on double layers of beaver skins, covered with birch bark leggings to keep their legs warm. Erick's hands were warm as toast, due in part to the warm fox skin mittens his mother had made him.

Erick knew they were close to his campsite. They just needed to stumble into it or into his woodpile. That didn't take more than a couple of seconds. They quickly secured themselves under Erick's protective lean-to. His firewood stack was completely dry under the protecting pine boughs.

Erick and Grandfather looked out from their camp at the hard driving snow. *I might not have caught fox or mink, but I sure made up for it with those two huge black bears,* Erick thought to himself.

It took only moments for them to have a blazing fire going. Their fire was so large in fact that snow began to melt from the boughs above them. The melting snow dripped down on their little oasis in the Lotorp wilderness. Grandfather put on coffee using the last coffee beans in the bottom of the glass jug that Erick had taken with him on the trip. Grandfather hung strips of beaver meat across the fire spit. Erick soon silenced his growling stomach with the beaver strips and the last bits of Swedish limpa bread that they shared as they laughed and talked. The taste of fresh coffee and delicious beaver strips along with the bread was almost too much for Erick to bear. Even Grandfather said that the beaver meal was filling, even if it wasn't home cooking.

Darkness set in around their little camp. Erick had been so very hungry from not eating all day and from pulling his two sleds and walking on cross-country skis that his eyes grew heavy. Erick and Grandfather both grew tired rapidly and began to nod off at the campfire while they talked. Erick almost pitched forward into the flames with his eyes closed. They cleared some snow from the forest floor and then laid out two woolen blankets in front of their fire. Building up their fire for the night, they finally climbed between the blankets. Grandfather glanced over at Erick with his mature, tired smile, and said simply, "Better than this there isn't." Cradling his rifle close to his chest, Erick was asleep in a second with not a care in the world.

They both awoke sometime before dawn. Erick rubbed his eyes and looked out across the creek. The snow had stopped along with the wind. They had survived the blizzard quite well. The blizzard had passed and the sky had turned a robin's egg blue, similar to a bright summer day.

Grandfather rekindled the fire and it quickly burst into bright flames. He didn't give much thought to the amount of wood he was using or how the snow was melting down upon them. All he could think of was taking Erick home. Erick made the fastest breakfast he had ever made or eaten. Grandfather helped pull Erick's nearly depleted food stock down from the tree. Grandfather calculated that they could be home in twelve to fourteen hours, providing they started right away. They would arrive long after dark. He figured that the family should still be awake, waiting for Grandfather to bring Erick home. After packing everything onto Erick's two sleds, they strapped on their skis. Grandfather took a large wax candle that he had brought and waxed both sets of snow skis before breakfast. They knew that waxing their skis would undoubtedly speed their long trip home.

Erick pulled his two sleds out onto the crusted deep snow. Grandfather pulled his sled carrying the first black bear sister behind Erick's sled. The bear was so large that its legs dragged along beside the sled on the snow crust. The seven-year-old was happier than he had ever been in his whole life. Erick leaned into the wind and held his rifle tight like a little toy soldier ready to do battle, whistling while he slid along on his skis. He felt so proud leading his grandfather home. Why shouldn't he be happy and proud? After all, the Namekagan men hadn't caught him and eaten him, the cougar hadn't mauled him, the badger couldn't kill him or his spirit, and the twin black bear sisters had their opportunity, but failed, even with their combined efforts. Erick's bones wouldn't be eaten clean by the timberwolves and the forest mice wouldn't be licking and feasting on Erick's bones this trip.

CHAPTER NINE

The little log cabin looked like a tiny speck in the distance. Erick was too exhausted to hurry. The deadly cold had blown in behind the blizzard as he expected it would, dropping the temperature well below zero. Grandfather could barely see because of the strong wind that forced him to squint. The rapid accumulation of drifting snow had now reached a depth that forced them to remove their skis and switch to snowshoes. They kept walking, putting one snowshoe after another.

As they got closer to the cabin, they saw the thin blue trail of smoke rising from the family's chimney. They smelled the fresh burning wood in the fireplace. A solid mist of blue smoke hung low over the little valley, the tall jack pine tops pierced the smoke, protruding like young asparagus tips out of a field. The pines looked like they rose through gentle billowing clouds. They were still a mile away and darkness had taken hold hours before. Erick's eyes welled up with tears as he moved closer. His heart pounded louder and his steps became faster. The two sets of snowshoes crunched along noisily on the high, fresh snow. As close as they could tell, there must have been two additional feet of snow since Erick had left home. Erick's muscles ached from twelve hours of pulling his two sleds. His feet felt blistered and his legs were in constant pain, with his knees throbbing.

Grandfather hollered out as they approached the fence line, "Johan, Anna, little Charles, we're home!"

It didn't take but a second for the cabin door to fly open and Erick's mother's full frame to fill the doorway. Mother was a fiery woman with thick legs like those on a piano. Her whole wardrobe consisted of two identical cotton print dresses: one for church and the other for everyday. Mother ran out into the cold and deep snow with only her house-dress and boots on. Erick wasn't sure which of the two dresses she was wearing,

She picked up Erick and hugged him so tight he thought his ribs would crack. He felt light-headed from her bear hug. She finally let him down but refused to let him go. She held him tight for what seemed like forever as her tears cas-caded down on him. Tears ran down Erick's dirty little face, rolling off his cheeks like a waterfall.

He couldn't believe that his mother was out in the snow with no coat or hat. She had always been so reserved about such things. Here she was standing in deep snow, crying, "My little boy, my little Erick. I was so worried about you. I'm so mad at your father that we have not spoken for days. All because he sent you away to do a man's job, and you're only a little boy." With that explanation she once again burst into tears. Grandfather said that Mother was wound up tighter than a eight-day clock. Mother swept Erick up press-ing him tightly to her bosom. Her dress had a strong smell of lye soap from being recently washed. She held him tight and proceeded to carry him to the open cabin door.

Little Charles was hanging onto the big pine door hop-ing to see his big brother, the trapper, for the first time in a week. Mother twisted Erick sideways to get him through the open doorway, since he was still wearing his snowshoes.

With Erick tucked under one arm like a sack of potatoes, she burst through the doorway into the cabin. Father was sitting up on the edge of his bed, tears in his eyes, crying without stop. He whooped, whistled, and applauded while continuing to weep. Erick unstrapped his snowshoes and ran over to Father as little Charles clung to one of his legs. Neither Father nor Erick said a word, holding each other close and tight until both of their tears completely soaked Erick's shirt.

Johan Holm was a quiet, simple man of few words until this day. Due to his pain, Father laid back down on his bed. After a few minutes, Father managed to lift up on one elbow, only to start crying again. Father had never cried before, or at least not in Erick's or little Charles' presence. Mother asked Grandfather if she could get him anything to eat. Grandfather jokingly said, "Don't fix anything special for me, a crust of bread is more than good enough for me." Grandfather had cleverly managed to bring a smile to Mother's distraught face.

After hours of storytelling and what must have been gallons of coffee along with fresh cream, everyone decided that it was time to go to sleep. The single kerosene lamp was blown out and a sour smell from the burnt kerosene settled across the room. Erick promised to tell more of his stories, adventures, and near-death experiences in the morning. The little cabin grew quiet. Warmth settled over Erick and he fell fast asleep in his little bed in the corner of the room.

Erick didn't know that while he slept the night away, his mother never left his side. She had pulled a chair over close to his bed and had slept there through the night. Johan Holm was sitting at the table when Erick awoke. Mother was making a big homecooked breakfast for her trapper, Erick, little Charles, Father, and Grandfather Ernst. Brim, mylsa, Swedish limpa bread, herring, apple butter, the table was bursting with all Erick's favorites. He couldn't believe his eyes but his nose told him it must be true. Breakfast would have to wait a moment. There was an immediate emergency. Erick clambered out of bed, dressed quickly, and took his porcelain chamber pot, which was quite full from his night of coffee drinking, and bolted to the outhouse to empty it down the two-seater.

Father looked greatly improved during the week Erick had been gone. He said he could breath a lot better and when he took each breath his ribs didn't hurt as much. Without a doctor, they could only guess at what the problem had been or what damage had been done. After all, Father had taken a terrible fall down an embankment after he had lost his footing. He had tumbled and rolled to a sudden stop against an unforgiving pine tree. Father had laid there for the better part of a day, barely able to breathe, his body shuddering from the bone deep cold that had penetrated to his soul. He lay there thinking his lung had collapsed and that he'd broken some ribs. Father knew he had been in and out of consciousness throughout his ordeal. It wasn't until Mother had gone to look for him that she discovered him lying against the trunk of a sixty-foot tall pine tree.

His healing had taken months of constant bed rest in the little cabin of logs and mud. The Holm family had made untold sacrifices for close to five months while Father was confined to his bed. Their meager savings had evaporated first and fast. Then slowly, one by one, the farm animals had been sold. There had only been two exceptions, Ole and Sven, the oxen. Mother had had to sell their prize milk cow too. With father disabled and bedridden, there was no one to tend the fields. Without constant cultivation, the fields had turned to weeds. No harvesting meant no hay, oats, or straw to feed the animals. All Mother could do was pick the unappetizing potatoes that lay in the fields and they too were pretty sparse. The potato fungus disease that had spread through Sweden in the 1840s had left the farmers with virtually nothing left to grow.

Since Erick's return from trapping with no furs to sell or trade, another dilemma had been thrust onto the Holm family. There was now a real probability of them starving to death. With no furs and no ability to sell any of the damaged pelts, life as they once knew it would soon come to a screeching halt. There would be no milk from the cow, no chickens for eggs, no wheat for bread, and no milk for butter. Everything looked bleak and hopeless. The Holm farm, for the first time in Erick's lifetime, seemed threatened. The family didn't own it; they only rented it from Old Man Nelson. Mr. Nelson lived over at the northern outskirts of Lotorp. He only had one big hairy left eyebrow. According to stories bandied about, the second eyebrow had been burned off by an out of control kerosene lamp. Every time Erick saw Mr. Nelson, it was all he could do not to burst into laughter. Mr. Nelson would certainly expect his money due for the rental of the farm. All the family had were Erick's two sleds full of useless and worthless beaver pelts. It was certain that Mr. Nelson would not accept the destroyed beaver pelts as rental on the property.

Erick's failed trapping expedition definitely put the final nail in his family's coffin. But there would be a pot of gold at the end of the rainbow from Erick's trapping trip, and that was the beaver and black bear meat. In addition, the two huge black bear hides would fetch a tidy sum when brought into the Lotorp market square. A small ray of hope shined into their little cabin. Mother spoke up and said, "With all this meat, at least we have no chance of starving anytime soon." Father broke in and said, "Not for a little while, thanks to Erick." The four of them just sat at the small table and four chairs with little Charles running happily back and forth.

Erick closed his eyes and dreamily thought about Grandpa Ernst as if he were sitting there at the little table with them. Erick smiled as he remembered Grandpa Ernst telling his tales about almost every subject imaginable. Grandfather could be such a character. Erick smiled his broadest smile as he molded himself after his grandfather, his mentor. Grandfather's life became his stories and his stories were his life. They were alive and in full living color. Their creation illustrated the magnificent, sweeping life that was Grandfather's.

Grandfather had been a blacksmith in his early youth. He was custom made for the Swedish wilderness and he made his way in the Swedish countryside, blazing a trail from the twists and turns of his life.

Grandfather had two distinct sides. He was known for huge, ugly feuds with his lifelong farming neighbors. He could keep all that would listen captivated with his fiery and much ballyhooed orations. He would expound upon subjects about which he was well read. Erick knew Grandfather thought nothing of working long hard grueling hours planting, sowing, and growing his wheat that had replaced his potato fields. Sometimes sleep would elude him for nights due to his long farming hours. His personality was deeply complicated with a conflicting interior life. His loving charm, natural wit, verbosity, and passion made him bigger than life and hugely fascinating. Grandfather was known to make outrageous claims, go to absurd lengths, push the limits, and exceed all the expectations of his family and friends.

Grandfather placed high goals upon himself and those around him. He always wanted his family to be more steadfast, more stoic, more devoted, more loyal and, when circumstances called for it, more long suffering. This was a lot to live up to, and Father aspired to meet Grandfather's perpetual challenge. While he was disabled, Father would spend spectacular amounts of time dreaming up magnificent feats to accomplish in order to live up to his father's appetite of overwhelming expectations.

Grandfather, unbeknownst to most, was well read, self taught, and broadly intelligent on worldly things. He had an ability for memorizing nearly every book he read. He desired to devour every book he could lay his enormous farm hands on and he became fairly fluent in English. Grandfather once said he didn't think English had enough common insults, so he created his own. One such insult was calling people "first-rate second raters." He would pontificate until the wee small hours of the morning, provided he could capture a willing ear or two to listen. This required an endless supply of hot black coffee plus a clear path to the two-seater outhouse during his stories.

Grandfather offered an abundance of provocative details about himself, but only to family. To outsiders he managed to obscure the actual facts of his life in a cloud of rumor, mystery, speculation, and conjecture. His intuition told him that there had been advantages to being placed into backward circumstances. He felt a person just had to be clever enough to discover the advantages.

Grandfather had been raised in somewhat of a cosmopolitan family in backwoods Sweden. His life was complex and full of hardships, all of which he had come to view in pragmatic terms, as stepping stones for moving forward in life. Grandfather's view of life was that a successful person was someone flexible enough to understand that each event in life can prepare you for the next step or event, if you knew how to let it. Adversity forced its opponents to find new and creative ways of moving forward and onward.

He continuously tried to immerse Erick into Sweden's minuscule cultural life whenever the chance would present itself.

Grandfather refused to acknowledge what was happening in his beloved country. He tried to block from his mind the enormous exodus of his countrymen and women, academics, scholars, tradesmen, fishermen, and farmers like himself. He would bellow, "Like rats running off a ship." He was deeply affected by the exodus of friends and relatives leaving to go to the New Worlds of Australia and America. He viewed those leaving as quitters and charlatans in a land of abounding numskullery and quackeries, of course with the exception of his son and his son's family.

Grandfather became revered, not so much by what he had done, but for who he was. Grandfather always dreamed of writing "The Big Book," or, with his broken Swedish accent, he would say, "Za Beek Buka," as it came out in Holm's elocution. It would be his El Dorado, his Holy Grail, his pot of gold at the end of the Swedish rainbow. He never did write the book!

Erick would try at times to fashion and mold himself after his grandfather, like some children would pretend they were cowboys and Indians or little girls would cut out paper clothing for their dolls.

CHAPTER TEN

Erick retreated from his dreamy thoughts of Grandfather Ernst and snapped back to reality.

Breakfast, lunch, and dinner had been eaten at the little farm table in the family's cabin. Family discussions and school homework were done around the same table. And, when their grandparents would stop over, the children would give up their places at the table and would sit either on the floor or on their beds. When Grandfather Anders Anderson Bostrom and Grandmother Brita Bostrom, along with Grandfather Ernst and Grandmother Anna would stop to say hello, everyone knew it was storytelling time. Either Father or one of the grandfathers would tell their stories.

Thousands of delicious meals had been eaten on the rickety old farm table. At one time or another, neighbors and church members had sat around the table, reading scriptures from their family bibles that they would carry everywhere. Around the same table, each and every decision about the farm or the family had been discussed and acted upon.

Erick felt a pang of uneasiness settle into his body, for he knew the final fateful decision about the family farm could and would be made around the old farm table with the wobbly legs. Erick's family knew the beaver and bear meat could only last them until early spring, with most of the bear meat being sold off immediately. Their last pig, which had been slaughtered right before Erick left to go trapping, would by week's end only be a pleasant memory of a delicacy gone by.

It was Sunday and Erick knew Grandfather Ernst and Grandmother Anna would be stopping by after church services. In the winter months, Grandmother Anna always brought homemade apple butter cookies for the whole family and in the summer months she would bring different berry pies every week. Excitement pulsated through Erick's taste buds anticipating the knock on the door that announced Grandfather and Grandmother and the mouth-watering cookies. Following the cookies, decisions would be made at the little table.

The loud knock finally came at the cabin door. The cookies had arrived and, of course, the grandparents too. Laughter filled the cabin to bursting. Erick told his stories of his trapping adventures and the destruction of all the beavers. He told about the badger, wolves, and twin black bear sisters. As his grandparents asked to hear more stories, Erick neglected to mention a word about falling through the ice into Potato Creek. Erick shuddered to think of his mother finding out. He pictured Mother's eyes becoming a dark stormy blue and her brows turning together in a scowl. He could imagine her with her feet spread wide apart and her hands on her hips, shaking her head and screaming at him, "Don't lie to me young man." Erick did know that the story about the twin black bear sisters had been whispered about from one end of the village to the other already. On hearing the story, people would announce that it was unbelievable, ungodly, and undeniably true. It was one of the biggest stories bandied about in years. Only Erick and Grandfather knew the true story. The true story of the danger he had faced was simply a small detail his parents and grandparents did not have to worry about unnecessarily. Besides, if they knew, he knew he would never be allowed to hunt and trap alone again. Following all Erick's stories came his father's story of the failing farm. Everyone realized the farm was in trouble, but no one imagined the magnitude of the failure. Erick's father was a farmer first. The rest of his time he spent as a blacksmith who also had quite a talent for hunting and trapping.

Each member of the family took turns speaking. One by one, as Erick and little Charles sat on the edge of the bed, they heard all the reasons why Father and Mother should not give up the farm. Mother said, "What we lack in our heads, we shall make up for with our hands in the New World." This was the first time Erick had heard his parents mention the New World that he knew to be North America. Then finally, it was Grandfather Ernst's turn to speak. Erick realized when Grandfather raised himself up from the rickety old chair and cleared his throat that a story was about to be heard. Grandfather, in Erick's eyes, was as rough as pine bark but could be as soft as a kitten. Grandfather would always walk and circle the room as he told one of his stories.

Erick bit down hard on another apple butter cookie in anticipation of another of Grandfather's stories. Mother put additional logs on the fire as Grandmother poured all of their coffee cups as full as she could. Grandfather bent down over Erick's bed and whispered, "Erick, if you keep drinking all that coffee, you won't grow any taller and won't be able to hunt down that badger of yours." Grandfather took a few steps over to the fireplace, struck a match on a fieldstone, and lit his pipe. The sweet smell of the tobacco drifted across the little cabin like a storm cloud.

As the patriarch of the Holm family, Grandfather Ernst began, "I feel obligated to finally get this off my chest and tell everyone the true story of the Swedish famine.

"It was the beginning of the horror. I beheld with sorrow one wide wasteland of putrefying vegetation throughout the countryside. Our wretched farming neighbors seated on the fences bitterly viewing their decaying gardens, wringing their hands and bewailing the horrendous destruction that had left them with no food for family or beast. As months passed, all the vegetation grew steadily worse. Men, women, and children all began to bloat. As I passed cottages, I noticed children bloated by the roadside, their mouths green from the grass they had eaten in an overpowering hunger that took over their minds and bodies. Whole families simply dropped dead after indulging in a simple meal of porridge, which would prove to be too much for their stomachs that had long suffered without food. Women slung their dead husbands onto their backs, staring blankly ahead on their way to the graveyards. Dogs fed on their half buried owners, and rats tore people to pieces who, though still alive, remained too weak to cry out. There were many villagers who became frantic, eating diseased livestock, chickens, and even human flesh. They called it the great famine, the event that helped shape our Swedish history.

"This famine reduced the Swedish population by millions in those famine years after 1840. Our potato, which had been the staple food of most of the Swedish population since the late sixteenth century, had been struck by an airborne virus. Within months the oppressive stench of black and decaying tubers filled the blackened fields across the landscape. Swedes were passing away in great numbers and the graveyards were filling at an alarming rate. Some simply walled themselves into their cottages and anxiously awaited the end of their lives. Many, weakened by hunger, succumbed to dysentery, typhus, and cholera while others crowded aboard ships, seeking salvation abroad in Canada, America, and Australia. Some survived and others passed away in the stinking holds of the 'coffin ships,' as they were called. Tens of thousands perished at sea or in the infamous Canadian quarantine stations."

Grandfather Ernst stopped his story short of the finish as his pipe had gone out from lack of tobacco. After refilling his pipe and striking another match on the fieldstones, the story resumed. Grandfather told how thirty percent of the Swedish population had been lost to starvation and disease while another thirty percent had been lost to emigration. The tragedy overwhelmed the government. It did not have the ability or know-how to cope with a disaster of such magnitude.

Grandfather continued, "It was indeed a hopeless event and the Swedish government simply turned their backs on the massive predicament. This has been one subject the Swedes have not talked about, as if possibly we older people would somehow forget about the famine. It has been too painful, too horrific, and too difficult to explain, because in many ways, none of it made any sense. So as the years have passed the topic has been dealt with by stoic silence. It has been an untold secret for years, for it severely wounded our country and dramatically changed the countries of Canada, Australia, and America, through an enormous influx of immigrants." Erick had heard this story time and again at school, but as Grandfather told the story, it took on a whole new meaning. Erick's blood ran cold as Grandfather finished his story. Tears ran down both of Grandmother's cheeks, as they must have known what was about to take place. Certainly Erick's grandparents must have discussed this time and again.

Father leaned forward grasping his coffee cup so hard it nearly shattered from the pressure of his massive farm hands. Father said ever so slowly and with no hesitation, "Mother and I have decided to immigrate to North America." A collective gasp was heard around the little table. Grandmother spilled her coffee over the edge of the table and it dripped down onto the floor planks.

It seemed as if everyone began to speak at the same time. Tears from all four grandparents fell on the little table in the corner of the room. Erick and little Charles began to weep together on the bed's edge. Erick sat with a shocked expression on his face. He had never heard anything about immigration before. He thought it must have all come about from his misguided trapping trip. Erick felt that the family's decision to go to the New World had to be his fault and his fault alone. How else could this have come to be? Johan said simply, "We think we will sell our possessions for passage money." All four grandparents began to cry once again. This was the end of the Holm family as they had always known it to be. Johan told his father that after they arrived and were settled in North America, they would send for all the grandparents.

CHAPTER ELEVEN

So it would be. Laughter had long stopped as tears continued to flow. The decision was made, the outcome anything but certain. In 1886, to escape famine and starvation, Johan Holm, his young wife, Anna, their three-year-old son, Charles, and their seven-year-old son, Erick, would leave Sweden for North America. Leaving the grandparents behind would prove to be the biggest hardship. Leaving all Erick's school friends, neighbors, and church members would also prove hard.

The church had always been a rock solid part of the Holm family. Even before the family could sell their personal and farm possessions, they had to approach their church minister and congregation in order to receive the church's approval and blessings before beginning the actual move.

Any and all family moves had to be condoned and approved by the church. All family movement into or out of the church, as well as each and every birth, baptism, and death, had to be recorded into the official church records. Swedish laws required this recordkeeping.

Approval was given to the Holm family without objection and was thusly recorded in church documentation as "immigrated to North America, February 1886." The Holm family members, from their earliest beginnings, came from the little villages of Norrkoping, Noppeming, Risinge, Hallingberg, and Lotorp. These little villages were in southeastern Sweden. Erick was born in Risinge and the family moved to Lotorp when he was an infant. Norrkoping was the nearest marketplace to sell farm animals and crops. It was also the only known market for fur trading that was within a day's journey by yoke of oxen. This proximity was important to be able to return home the same day. Fur trading was as important or possibly more important than the fish markets that sprung up every Saturday morning. Potatoes were the backbone of the vegetable crop in these farming communities. Southern Sweden was, after all, the breadbasket of the whole country.

There were also water sources wherever you looked in Sweden. In every direction you traveled, there were lakes, streams, brooks, canals, seas, and oceans. If someone didn't like to eat fish, potatoes, or wild game, they would rapidly grow quite thin. Potatoes were the main crop. The famine and drought began in 1845 and by 1846 the harvested potatoes were the size of peas. If a man were diligent with his farming, he could feed his family but he'd have no crops left to sell at market. The potato famine lasted off and on until 1860. By the end of the second year of the famine, families were leaving Lotorp and surrounding towns and villages by the hundreds.

It was during the fourteen years of the famine that the Holm family's uncles, aunts, and cousins immigrated to North America. It had always been the custom for men to leave first. They would immigrate to wherever they could book passage. These hardy men would almost always gain employment as foresters, lumberjacks, or railroad workers. They would live together in shantytowns or tarpaper shacks. In this way, by personally sacrificing, they saved their money to bring their wives and children over to begin a new life together.

Word had spread through Lotorp like a wildfire about the wonderful opportunities in North America. Stories came back that America had great forests as far as the eye could see and further than a Swede could travel by foot in a month. With these forests, they were told, Swedes could build log cabins and cottages as they had done in Sweden. Letters coming back from North America promised abundant supplies of wood to heat their cabins and build livestock barns. Stories were told that if you cleared a parcel of land and built a cabin on that cleared piece of land, you could someday own that piece of property, with no landlord to pay as it had been in Sweden. There were eyewitness reports of fish so large in the fresh water lakes that they could eat a small child.

With all these wild stories of North America floating through Erick's mind, he thrilled at the possibility of a voyage on the sea and ocean. Grandmother's eyes were red from crying, but her tears had finally stopped. She passed the cookies around the table one last time, saying, "How much longer are we going to wallow in our daily suffering?" Father reached over and held his mother's hand and said, "Our suffering days are numbered here in Sweden." Mother asked Grandfather and Grandmother to give some thought to immigrating along with them to North America.

"Oh my, oh my, how could we possibly go and leave our farm, our church, neighbors, and family?" Grandmother said, once again beginning to cry.

But grandfather, with his eyes glassy, tried to hold back a tear that had still managed to escape. The tear was impossible to stop as it fell down upon the little wobbly table. Grandfather said, "Let's not be so hasty, Grandmother." He looked directly into Erick's eyes. Grandfather admired his grandson, who he called his young warrior. "We shall spend time thinking about it, as our hearts would break without our loving family remaining together." That was wonderful news to Erick. It was a glimmer of hope that his grandparents would follow them to North America. So it was that Father, Mother, Erick, and little Charles made their biggest decision to leave Sweden.

CHAPTER TWELVE

Erick adored his father. He found him to be the embodiment of force and fervor. Therefore, young Erick thrilled at the thought of a voyage on the ocean with him. He had only heard stories about the ocean but had never ever seen it. He also knew virtually nothing about money except that his mother and father had none to speak of. Erick asked his parents, "If we have no money saved, how can we travel and pay our tickets for passage?"

Father explained, "We have a few farm animals to take to market and we shall also sell our farming tools and implements."

With that answer Erick seemed satisfied and he stopped asking questions, except for one last one. Erick asked, "How did the famine begin that has caused us to leave our farm and country?"

Mother slowly spoke, trying to explain the reason to Erick. She explained it to him as it had been told to her, "It began as an airborne virus that rotted the potato plants as they fruited, and that quickly spread all across the country."

Grandfather broke in to continue, "The Swedish population had become totally dependent on its potato for nutrition. With the potato crops blackened, farmers lost their income and a major source of food, with the exception of fish. Now families couldn't afford to buy or trade for other food such as corn, grain, and meat. Cattle and hogs were used to pay landlords for renting the farms and then exported for maximum monetary payments. Rate collectors were turned away, sometimes forcibly. So with no potatoes to eat, little help from the outside world and neighboring countries, Swedes began to starve to death despite the fact that Swedish seaports burst with vessels laden with food for England and Europe. Sweden was not singled out as the only country to be struck by the rotting plants and famine. There were contiguous countries like Ireland, Scotland, Germany, and Poland.

"Rate collectors told of tragic tales. In some houses, rate collectors found the corpses of whole families dead, in many cases, for quite some time. Some houses and cottages were completely deserted. Along the ditches were bodies badly mangled by animals and household pets. The poor creatures that were still alive were but living ghosts. Before the famine, Swedes were some of the healthiest people in the world. They ate potatoes, supplemented by milk and honey. This was a mono-diet but it sustained them. This in addition to the fish had kept them a powerful nation of athletic people. Then came the famine, which not only destroyed lives, families, entire villages, but it also destroyed their values, which they had prided themselves on.

"The Swedish peasantry had been a communal society, but the famine destroyed their sharing and giving natures. They could no longer help their neighbors because they had nothing even for themselves. The Swedes were humiliated by this new situation. The first Swedes that went to North America did not talk at all about the famine once they got there. In this way, the story about the famine was not passed down from generation to generation. Six thousand miles distance made it easier to block the whole famine out of

their minds and lives. So, soon our great-grandfathers simply said nothing. The famine became the shameful secret in
all the Swedish families.

"When word of the famine got out, there were three
groups in America that responded and wanted to help. The
first to arrive in Sweden were the Quakers, who rushed in to
set up soup kitchens. Then came the Jews along the eastern
seaboard, also setting up food kitchens. Finally, the
Choctaw Indians, who had themselves suffered starvation
when being forcibly moved by the American government
from their homelands to a reservation in Oklahoma. This
was the famous 'Trail of Tears,' and they did not forget the
pain and suffering. The Choctaws voted to donate their
entire treasury of $170.00 to the starving in Sweden."

Mother opened up her book that she kept next to the
family bible. "Erick," she said softly, "this is a poem I mem-
orized from when I went to school and kept it as a remem-
brance of the famine." She read, "Live skull, blind-eyed,
balanced on wild higgledy-piggledy skeletons, scoured the
land in forty-five, wolfed the blighted root and died."

The Holms had little to no money, as it had been several years since any crops had been saleable. The one major
asset they did have was their stock of farm animals that had
gotten through the blight years unscathed. They also had
barrels of seed potatoes which they had been afraid to plant
for fear they too would fall victim to the disease.

So it began. The process of uprooting the family and
migrating to America began, as it had for tens of thousands
of Swedish families before them. The family's ultimate
decision could no longer be kept a shadowy secret. It was
decided to go forward and tell the members of their church
congregation first, for they felt that would be the hardest
part. The congregation elders seemed to take the news
extremely well. There was no wailing or fainting as the

family had expected. Actually the members of the church said that they had been expecting the news for quite a long period of time. Records at the church were brought out in preparation for the final date of leaving the congregation and the actual signing of the document. The little Lutheran church in Lotorp was a beehive of activity. Johan and Anna were at the center of several conversations after their announcement about leaving for North America.

Now it was time for the true test and that was disposing of all the years of personal items along with toolsheds full and a barn packed with the necessities of farming. They spread the word as best they could for the times they lived in, but word got out at a snail's pace. It was the beginning of February, the shortest month of the year. So much had to be done and details had to be worked out in order to coincide with the all-important sailing season. If things dragged slowly and not as predicted, the whole plan would fall apart piece by piece, and they could ill afford any problem as they neared their leaving. Seven days went by, then fourteen, and no one bought any of the items that were for sale. By the end of the third week, panic struck the family. It was the end of February and nothing had sold. That Sunday, Johan and Anna stood up in front of their church congregation. Father announced they would have an immigration sale the following Sunday afternoon. They explained that everything would and must be sold. The wheels were set into motion. Charles fidgeted and carried on terribly, constantly tugging on his mother's finest church dress, actually, her only dress. Erick stood erect next to his father's leg, tall and proud as a boy could be at seven years old. Erick knew that each and every member of the congregation had heard of his brave ordeal out in the Lotorp woods. Pride filled his small chest, because he knew he had helped his family get through the winter. To insure a fine turnout at their sale, Father announced that refreshments would be served. The sale would follow the church service the next Sunday.

That Sunday after church, it seemed like every neighbor and friend came from near and far to the Holms' sale. Reverend William Olson and his wife, Diana, along with their children, Timothy, Andrew, and Doris, were the first to arrive. Reverend Olson said a prayer and blessed the food. Personal belongings, tools, farming implements, and farm animals were all sold with little or no bartering on prices. Money was exchanged, tears flowed like a spring rain, good-byes were said, hugs were exchanged, and the sale was completed. With beds and bedding all sold, furniture loaded on wagons and carts, all the friends, neighbors, and church members pulled away from the Holm farm. That night the family curled up in front of the fireplace and fell asleep quickly after such a full and exhausting day.

CHAPTER THIRTEEN

Early the next morning, the Holm family placed their meager belongings onto their yoke of oxen. Two hundred pounds of seed potatoes were loaded first, and then fifty pounds of pickled pike plus little Charles and they were on their way to North America. They traveled south from Lotorp to Vaxjo then to Linkoping. They followed the shore of Sweden's great Lake Vattern and they rested. They had come quite some distance and were close to Jonkoping at the southern tip of Lake Vattern. The family had been walking for days and was tired and exhausted.

With nothing to do but walk, Erick simply watched the clouds that had been forming throughout the day. The little white puffy clouds had given way to bigger gray and black clouds. Father kept the oxen and family moving as the huge menacing clouds seemed to settle directly over their heads. Suddenly, lightening flashed across the rutted road. There was a loud clap of thunder that echoed across the open fields and forest. The thunder boomed louder and louder.

Little Charles started to cry, so Mother picked him up and carried him as the family walked. They never stopped except to eat and sleep. Then it happened; lightening struck a nearby oak tree on the forest's edge. Flaming branches flew and wood splinters and sparks sprayed down close.

Thunder boomed again, only this time it began to rain like cats and dogs. It started as a cold gentle rain. They didn't have to wait long until the gentleness of the rain turned into a hard driving rain. They all looked like drowned rats in a matter of minutes. If that wasn't hardship enough, the wind came up out of the northwest. The wind blew harder and harder as little Charles cried louder and louder. The wind grew cold and the cold rain turned to sleet.

They plodded on through the now muddy road. It didn't take long until the sleet turned to snow, but not a light fluffy snow. A heavy wet snow began to fall and now each step forward was an effort. The rutted road was deep with water and the heavy snow just lay down on the ruts like a heavy blanket of wool. The snow stuck to everything and everyone. Their cart was solid white, as were their oxen. Little Charles' crying had been replaced by a slow methodical whimpering and whining. Each step forward was now a footstep into deep muddy slush. As the snow came cascading down on them, there was another clap of thunder. Lightening flashed across the sky and hit with a violent crash less than a hundred yards to the north.

Father looked for cover. They had been following a road around Lake Vattern. Father saw a cabin ahead and said, "Let's go to the cabin for shelter." The cabin was old, really old, close to falling down old. The door swung open as Father gave it a slight push. It swung open only to fall off its rusted hinges and crash to the floor. Father walked in first. Everyone stood outside the open doorway in the freezing rain. Mother didn't want to go any further. She stood strong and defiant as if guarding the doorway so no one could get in or out.

Little Charles was wrapped tightly in her arms. The only sounds were the sounds of his whimpering. Mother finally stepped inside after much coaxing from Father to do so. The cabin was small and box-like with an open loft. It measured about twelve feet square. It could have been a hunter or trapper's cabin or even a poacher's cabin.

As their eyes grew accustomed to the darkness of the cabin, Mother pointed to a corner where an old relic of a potbelly stove stood. An old rickety flue pipe extended up through the roof. It seemed like everyone spoke at the same time. "Let's make a fire!" This must have been their lucky day because next to the stove, stacked neatly in a pile, was dry firewood and a lot of it. Father started a fire and in minutes they began to feel the warmth from the potbelly. After a lot of pleading, Mother finally put little Charles down. The cabin grew light from the flames of the open potbelly. Father picked the cabin door up from the floor and leaned it against the door opening. It was hardly home, but they were out of the rain and were getting warmer by the minute.

With the light from the flickering stove, they could see the contents of the cabin. Over against the wall closest to the potbelly was a set of old bunk beds. There was no bedding or pillows but how wonderfully welcome those beds looked. Two chairs beckoned to Mother and little Charles to sit down, which they did. There against another wall was a small table with a leg that had fallen off and just lay there waiting for someone to screw it back on. A washbasin sat on the table with a porcelain pitcher for water. Now they knew they were not alone as the basin had many droppings in it. The cabin had one small window but no panes of glass, only an old oilcloth covering it. Father pulled back the oilcloth briefly to look out, only to see it raining even harder. They could hear the rain pounding on the roof. They found it hard to believe that the roof of the old cabin didn't leak. A small shelf held a few fishhooks, some lead fishing weights, and an assortment of droppings. Now the family was warm as toast and to some degree comfortable.

Darkness fell on the little cabin and they decided they would definitely stay the night.

The storm didn't sound like it would be letting up anytime soon. Mother agreed that they should stay at least until the rain stopped, even if it meant staying another day. Erick and little Charles were very excited. After all, no one wanted to travel in the rain and mud. Father went out to tether the oxen to a tree for the night. At the same time, he brought in a loaf of hard bread along with some apple butter. The little cabin was wonderful, especially after they had eaten the whole loaf of bread. The family was exhausted from walking through the mud for hours. Their clothes were dry thanks to the potbelly's heat, so they all decided to go to bed. Father climbed up on the top bunk but only to check it for safety for the boys. He came down and said, "Who wants to sleep up on the top?" Little Charles and Erick clambered up onto the top bunk and were asleep in moments. Father and Mother took the remaining lower bunk after Father had built up the fire for the night. They all slept like babies.

The family was awakened at dawn by the screaming sounds of their oxen. Father flew out the door only to be confronted by a menacing cougar circling the oxen. The oxen were trapped against the tree that Father had tethered them to. The cougar was snarling and then he let out a blood-curdling cry that sent Father into a rage. Father was screaming at the cougar at the top of his lungs. The cougar's three-foot tail just swung back and forth as he decided what he was going to do about Father. The cougar began to circle the oxen again, ever so slowly, disregarding Father completely as Father had no weapons. The cougar hissed and bared his teeth again; he was coming in for the kill. With all Father's screaming and the cougar's screaming, everyone had come to the open doorway. Father had no gun because it had been sold at the sale, so he just stood there screaming in a futile attempt to scare the cougar away, but that wasn't working.

Erick saw movement out of the corner of his eye and he heard Mother say, "Get out of the way, boys." With that Mother picked up the door that Father had placed against the opening. She burst through the doorway carrying the door like a warrior carries a lance. Mother had taken control of the situation. The cougar saw Mother running straight at him with that door. Father quickly got out of Mother's way because she was bent on running off that cougar. Father just stood there in disbelief as Mother ran by him with the door lowered in a frightening manner. Seeing Mother running at him, the cougar bolted and ran into the nearby woods and out of their lives. A cheer rang out from the family. Father gave Mother a giant hug and the children came running barefoot through the mud to join in the family celebration. Erick asked, "Do you think that was the same cougar that harassed me on my trapping trip?" Father said, "It could certainly be the same one."

With the sun about to come up in a beautiful blaze of color, they decided to leave right after breakfast. The rainstorm had passed them during the night and it looked like the day would be dry for traveling. The oxen must have felt a weight had been lifted off since the cougar was no longer a threat. Father too was relieved that the cougar's threat had passed. Father knew that if the cougar had killed the oxen, they would have had to pull the cart themselves, and to do that they would have had to unload the barrels of seed potatoes and pickled pike due to their extreme weight.

The sun was beginning to rise through the woods. A day without rain or snow would be a blessing, but they still would have the thick tar-like mud to contend with. Father tended the oxen and hooked them back onto the cart.

Mother fixed a fabulous breakfast on the potbelly stove, her famous family favorite, "lost bread," a form of French toast.

Erick had been walking around the outside of the cabin when he discovered that Lake Vattern was only thirty feet from the little cabin. The wind was blowing up from the lake and the lake's waves were breaking along the rocky shoreline. It didn't take long for the waves to turn into massive white caps that pounded even harder onto the rocks.

Erick thought, "What a great place for a fishing cabin. Only a few feet from the water's edge, nothing could be any better than this for any fishermen." Erick went back into the cabin only to discover little Charles had crawled back up into the bunk bed. Mother was slicing into a second loaf of bread and putting the thick slices onto the tip of a hickory stick. When asked where she had found the stick, she told Erick they were over in the corner next to the bunks. Erick looked for and found another hickory stick. He too decided to place a slice of bread onto the tip. They held their bread over the flames in the potbelly until they became a golden brown. It wasn't long before everyone was eating toast on a stick and laughing loudly over their early morning adventures.

After breakfast, Father gathered water from the lake using the old pitcher and put the fire out in the potbelly. He leaned the door back up over the opening and Mother gave the old door a light kiss, thanking the door for warding off the cougar and possibly saving the lives of their oxen. The boys said their fond farewells to the little cabin in the woods. It had served them well and they were thankful that the cabin had found them.

Once again, they started to walk along the rutted road toward the North Sea and a ship awaiting their arrival. They continued walking along the southern tip of Lake Vattern, now heading toward Jonkoping. Traveling west, they slowly pushed and pulled their cart through mile after mile of rutted muddy roads. As the miles added up, they seemed to walk slower and slower. Their days of travel had been exhausting. From time to time, they would come across other travelers on the rutted road made of mud. The Holms would stop to pass on stories with the travelers and in so doing heard stories from them. All these days of walking through, in many cases, knee-deep mud had taken a terrible toll on their clothing and shoes. Erick and Father were the only ones wearing boots, but it really didn't matter. Shoes or boots, they had all fallen apart and come apart at the seams. They stopped often along the route to do shoe repairs. Mother was appointed official shoe repairer. All she could do was wrap cloth around the gaping holes in their shoes and boots. All of their feet were swollen, bleeding, and blistered. Mother had been keeping little Charles from crying by constantly promising him a piece of licorice once they arrived at the marketplace.

That evening they camped out under the stars as usual, but something was noticeably different. Lying there under the stars, they, for the first time in any of their lives, breathed in the fresh smell of sea air blowing down on them from the west. Father told them that they must be closer than they thought. Mother said, "Thank heavens." As hearty as she was, her feet felt like they were going to give out on her. Mother was a robust, slightly heavy woman who actually weighed more than father. Her weight probably had an effect on her blistered feet. Morning came and once again they started out after breakfast. As they walked straight west into the sea breeze that was now very strong, father said suddenly, "Do you smell that? That's the smell of fish." Moments later, they heard seagulls and saw them flying in circles above them.

Chapter Fourteen

Fresh seawater air filled their lungs and the smell of fish was overpowering to the farming family. All they had ever smelled before was cultivated earth and barn animals. Directly ahead lay the Göteborg docks and the city of Göteborg.

As they came closer, they saw sailing ships as far as their eyes could see. The ships were docked along an enormous waterfront with rows of storefronts and brothels. These stores sold everything known to man and even a few things unknown to farming families.

Father stopped to ask where the Göteborg market was located. He knew the family was hungry and thirsty. It was late afternoon and they were too hungry to go looking for ships destined for North America. They followed some directions from an old salt that was walking past them. He told them the market was just over a rise and down a slight incline. Even though it wasn't far, it was too far for Mother's swollen and blistered feet. The marketplace was still open so they bought fresh fruit, which they had not seen in months, plus some promised licorice for the boys, fresh bread from the bakery, and homemade grape jelly. The good food made them feel they had reached heaven.

After eating, they pulled their cart over to a tree-lined and secluded area where they could camp again under the stars. There was no rain and it wasn't very cold. They huddled together to keep warm and went to sleep. Father kept thinking about the next day and scouting for a ship to North America. The night was restless for the whole family. After all, the following day could be their last day on Swedish soil. Morning would bring a whole new way of life for these Swedish farmers.

After a breakfast of leftover fresh bread bought from the market the night before, they headed back to the docks. Again, the ships were lined up neatly in rows. Not being able to tell which ships were arriving and which ships were departing, they had to make contact with each individual ship. They found out quickly that all the departure days and times were completely at the discretion of the ships' captains and any and all bookings were negotiated through the ships' first mates. They learned through negotiations that no promises were ever made as far as accommodations, length of travel, direction of travel, and there were no guarantees of a safe arrival. Each ship's first mate had about the same thing to say. They warned parents about hazards to the physical and emotional health of their children. Anyone with even the smallest degree of a health problem was warned not even to think about going on such a hazardous journey.

Father was truly upset about all the warnings. He said, "Maybe this trip is too dangerous."

Mother said, "We came this far, we can certainly go on a little boat ride."

Talking with a few seamen sitting along the docks gave new meaning to the words, "impending danger." The seamen told them that any voyage was considered physically and emotionally dangerous to the health of the young as well as the old. The seamen said that many of the young voyagers broke down mentally to the bewilderment of renowned Swedish psychiatrists. The seamen told stories of hundreds of voyagers going mad in the holds of the ships. From listening to these stories, many soon-to-be immigrants feared disaster was imminent. They turned around and headed home without ever getting onto a ship.

One seaman told Father about the brutality, beatings, and deaths on these ships. He spoke of all the different ways to die or be killed on what he called "the coffin ships." The sailor said they earned this nickname because the voyagers were put in large holds at the bottom of the ships that resembled coffins. He said some peasants who had just returned from North America or Australia were actually considered mad as they would climb up onto rooftops and deliver testimony of the atrocities they had seen, but almost no one would listen to them. After all, who would believe the ravings of a lunatic? The sailor went on to say that these madmen would have stories of being packed into filthy and suffocating coal rooms in the bowels of the ships and hearing screams of the immigrant peasants day and night without stop. Father asked the sailor why these ships were allowed to cruise from continent to continent without being subject to rules and regulations? He told Father that no rules or regulations existed. The sailor told of one villager he knew that had returned and that had become severely depressed. The villager told him, "Someone died inside of me, and that someone was me."

After speaking with these men of the sea, it seemed that all the ships had a dark side made up of dark days and months at sea. The decision was getting close at hand. It was time to pick which ship they would make their own. The Holm family knew nothing about ships. There were two-, three-, and four-masted ships, some steam-powered, some not. There were some that certainly did not look sea-worthy and probably should have been retired.

The family found out quickly that there was no such thing as an average fare of passage. Many Swedes simply negotiated with the ship's first mate for an agreed upon price. Crowds were on the docks day and night seeking passage. Many prospective passengers were not selective as to choice of ship or accommodations. When one actually selected a ship, the payment was made to the first mate. The first mate was a fast-talking, hard bargaining, and vigorous negotiator, whose fierce tactics always ended in additional gold or silver going into his pockets. After costs were settled, families were sent below deck into large crowded rooms called coal holds. Families and their farm animals shared the same accommodations. All these ships were called "human cargo coffins," or simply "coffin ships."

All the stories were the same. The immigrants lost all their dignity in a matter of hours. These despicable accommodations were called steerage. Steerage was the area located below sea level. Father found out that "steerage" meant you paid the lowest possible fare and received the most inferior lodging. Simply put, the humans would be sleeping with the animals. For payment clarity, your full family name was added to the passenger list. You were then given a receipt showing that you had made full payment, although the price was not documented. You were then instructed to go down the dock to a bedding storefront. There you selected your own mattress for the trip. These so-called mattresses were one gunnysack for children or two gunnysacks for adults. You then filled your sacks with clean, dry straw and that's how your mattress was made.

On these ships, whole families sat, ate, and slept on the bottom of the coal holds. Dignity, self-esteem, and pride were soon lost and replaced by barbarous acts, conditions, and attitudes. An uncivilized, mercilessly harsh culture soon took over from the refinement and churchgoing upbringing of these honest farm families. They had only one real goal: a better life, a life where they could feed their families. Though the Holms were certainly dirt poor, they more than made up for it in honesty, a trait that has followed generations of Holms to this day.

The Holm family had no passports or visas. This sort of problem was overlooked. Money, gold, or silver was substituted for lack of legal credentials. As it turned out, the Holm family was among those registered as undocumented, unauthorized immigrants. Each ship was filled to capacity with human cargo. There was no such thing as a normal passenger load. Steerage costs varied depending on the greed of those who ran the ships. That varied too depending on how close the ship was to leaving port.

The Holm family was impatient to leave since they had no housing and were living day-to-day from the back of an oxen-driven cart. The date of departure was critical, so they went ship to ship asking each ship's first mate or ranking crewmember when the ship was leaving. Most ships had a capacity of 350 passengers, though they would take fares for double that number. This was called overbooking. Unsuspecting passengers would board at a predetermined date and time. By the time they were herded down into the bowels of the ship, it was too late to get their money back and, for most, too late to even get off the ship.

Göteborg was the largest departure point in Sweden and also the shortest distance to the New World. Therefore, leaving from Göteborg meant paying the cheapest fare of passage. The Holms could have traveled to Stockholm, which was closer to Lotorp, but too expensive for the fare. Swedish immigrants came from all over Sweden to Göteborg. Thousands like the Holms traveled from as far away as Stockholm. They came on foot, by carts and wagons, or rode farm animals, from east to west. An alternative to walking would have been to take the Gota Canal. That is a canal passing through Sweden's two great lakes, but it was undoubtedly costlier. Sweden was one of the largest countries in Europe. The Swedes were rugged and could endure tremendous hardships. These ancestors of Leif Ericson and his father, Eric the Red, were indeed fierce warriors.

CHAPTER FIFTEEN

The anchor of the ship the family chose was originally hoisted near Liverpool, England. In her lifespan, she would cross the treacherous North Atlantic a number of times. The original captain said she had the grace of a white swan on her maiden voyage. The ship was a combination of a steam sloop, which was a steam-operated coal burner, and semi-man-of-war. She was built in the industrial age. An iron chimney rose between her towering sails. She used her sails to conserve the precious coal stock.

She originally flew the English flag on her maiden voyage, but when she set sail with the Holm family aboard, she raised no flag of origin. That was no surprise to anyone, as she was carrying a full complement of illegals. Her galley had a copper chimney and was fueled with cords of hardwoods picked up at dockside.

One such monstrous purchase was ten Dahlgren cannons. Admiral John Adolph Dahlgren, an earlier Swedish immigrant, was the most noted designer of military ordnance used in the American Civil War. Two of Admiral Dahlgren's cannons were mounted side by side on the *Monitor*'s center beam, along with Swedish immigrant John Ericsson's revolving cannon turret. Admiral Dahlgren was a personal friend of America's president, Abraham Lincoln.

The *Monitor*'s captain, John Worden, was soon to become a naval legend. The ship was fitted with ten cannons. Her cannons were a pretext for defensive measures only. As a semi-man-of-war, it was nebulous as to being for protection only. The twin Dahlgren deck cannons and John Ericsson's revolving cannon turret had elaborate iron tracks that formed sliding mechanisms which could be used to pivot out her two revolving center beam cannons. This revolving cannon turret was hidden to the naked eye by oak barriers that folded away if the cannon was to be used.

In the 1860s to 1880s, mechanical and metallurgy technology grew in bursts of imagination, ingenuity and genius. From the time of the ship's christening through its numerous voyages, she would pick up new technology at dockside sales. The *Monitor* was the ironclad ship that halted the Confederate ship, *CSS Merrimac,* at Hampton Roads and changed naval history forever. The two had steamed up to each other and had become tight as ticks, circling in a deadly dance. Neither ship won their deadly duel.

Another Swede, John Ericsson, designed the screw for navigation as well as the ironclad gunboat, *Monitor*. This sea battle between *Monitor* and *Merrimac* did for the Union on water, what the battle of Gettysburg was later to do for the Union on land.

The ship the Holm family would board was built at John Laird and Sons, shipbuilders near Liverpool, England. She was christened and rolled into England's Mersey River. Her name was *Enrica*, taken from hundred-year-old records, but no proof has been found as to her true name. It was only one of three names she sailed under at different times. Her first voyage carried a party of ladies and gentlemen, which was normal for that time period. These were known as sea trials. She was built at a time when ships were transitioning from sails to steam power. She was created from the finest oaks.

Red, white, and black oak were the specifications on all
drawings. Her bottom was sheathed in copper, which was
highly unorthodox at the time. She was rigged as a three-
masted, square-rigged sailing vessel, but powered by coal
burning furnaces and twin horizontal steam engines. She
was capable of speeds up to thirteen knots. For better
streamlining, her funnel could be telescoped downward and
her propeller lifted free of the water to avoid drag while the
ship was under sail. This funnel and propeller technology
was in transition during this period.

Her captain, Lieutenant John Worden, was tall, over six
feet, barrel-chested, and broad shouldered. He had a full
moustache, along with salt and pepper hair that lay on his
shoulders. When he spoke, he had an amiable growl in his
voice. The first lieutenant, S. Dana Greene, or first mate, as
he was called, was also tall, but powerfully built with a full
beard unlike the captain's cropped beard. The beards were
calculated to underline their authority and to present to the
poor illegal peasants an intimidating appearance. When
seen together, the captain and first mate possessed a fierce
stature. Their passengers saw them as cruel and treacherous,
but resolute in character.

The first mate was totally in charge of every detail of
running the ship. His booming English accent resounded
across the deck in a perfect hurricane of profanity. He had
heavy dark eyebrows that raised and lowered like a draw-
bridge as he barked out orders to the crew. The first mate
made no distinction to race or color of human cargo. He
sent everybody and every living thing down to the coal
holds. There was no separation of animals and humans.

Father spoke softly so no one but Erick could hear, saying, "It's like an ethnic ghetto down here." It didn't take long
to find out that many Scandinavians were dumber than a
sack of herrings when it came to the ship and ocean travel.

The entire ship felt masterful and, as Erick looked over it, he had a feeling of grandeur. The ship had English registry papers but, as the Holms had already noted, it failed to hoist any flag of origin. This fact brought questions and concerns to the Scandinavian passengers, including the Holms. The ship's crew was a diverse assemblage of people that had been to nearly every port of call in the world. Most of the crew were incorrigible young rascals from Liverpool and some were the poorest set of green hands. Each member of the crew had signed individual contracts, or articles of agreement, in most cases with their mark or an X. These contracts ensured the captain that they were bound men and would return with him. Because so many were liars, thieves, swindlers, and worse, those same contracts were basically worthless scraps of parchment.

One main reason the captain had no trouble signing on a crew each trip was the reputation that followed him. The captain of this ship, Lieutenant John Worden, had proven his mettle in the American Civil War. He had moved up through the ranks to become the captain of the ironclad ship *Monitor.* He had served gallantly and successfully in battling Jefferson Davis' ironclad ship, *Merrimac,* known in the South as the *CSS Virginia.* He had been wounded with wood splinters in his eyes. President Abraham Lincoln had selected the captain personally as the greater war leader over many that had graduated with honors from Annapolis or West Point. He had selected the captain for his reservoirs of patience and humor and his lack of sympathy. President Lincoln once said to the captain, "I have placed you in command of the *Monitor,* and yet I think it is best for you to know that there are some things in regard to which I'm not quite satisfied with you. I do believe you to be a brave and skillful officer, which of course I like. You have confidence in yourself, which will be valuable, if not indispensable, and

now, beware of rashness, but with energy and sleepless vig-
ilance, go forward and give us victories."

The other side of the captain's warrior syndrome was his
studiousness. His only relaxation from the daily monotony
of running the ship was his being an avid reader. It was said
that he had brought one hundred books onboard with him,
along with one hundred pints of rum. His second mate, who
did all the navigational plotting and math for the course of
travel, made mention of the fact that the captain could recite
many of the books from cover to cover. He read book after
book in his quarters, which was strewn from end to end with
them. He had hysterical phrases that would ignite the crew's
sense of humor. One such phrase was, "If wishes were horses, then beggars would ride."

The captain was known to be abrasive with his crew, but
they overlooked this. The captain also made it a practice to
punish or dismiss men who failed to perform to his high
expectations. The crew would work like horses and live like
pigs. He was always exceptionally unforgiving as a leader
and officer, but his men would follow him into any battle,
partially due to his paternal air of concern. Each member of
his crew obeyed every order without hesitation.

He also had a widespread reputation for being more
than fair with his crewmembers in the more important matter of whiskey rationing. The ship's crew had a daily
whiskey ration that was dispensed at the end of each day.
Some sipped the whiskey and others simply threw it down
their throats. The ranking crewmembers dispelled every
emotion of fear as they were carry-overs from the American
Civil War and were hardened men who had seen every
aspect of war. The lesser-seasoned green crew who handled
the galley and coal furnaces were mostly dysfunctional liars
and wanted criminals. Each green hand was given a corn-

husk-filled mattress, called a donkey's breakfast, and was shown to the forecastle, where he would bunk.

On their day of departure, the Holm family sat on the dock watching ships in the distance, not knowing if they were arriving or departing. They saw several merchant vessels, whaling ships, and a man-of-war on the horizon. Coming into the harbor was a merchantman flying the American flag.

The weather all that day was gorgeous, with afternoon temperatures climbing into the forties. Father walked over to a group of old salts that were drinking in the clean fresh salt air. Father asked if they knew anything about the particular ship that they'd decided to board. An old retired sailor spoke up and started to tell Father about it. The sailor said that by 1880, the ship was beginning to deteriorate from years of voyages and was loose at every joint. He went on to say that her seams were open and the copper on the bottom was in havoc. She was long overdue for dry dock and extensive overhaul. But during years of mass immigration from Scandinavia there was a sad lack of maintenance to these human cargo ships. He said he knew the ship's weight to be about 1,030 tons, which was her christening weight. Father looked up at the deck as crewmembers chanted, "Let's go, let's go, for God's sake." They knew the quicker they set sail the quicker the whiskey rationing would begin.

The captain stood at the rail dressed in his military dress blues. He looked regal in comparison to his unkempt crewmembers. The captain announced that he would throw a festive party that evening, right before pulling out from the docks. He always did this to ensure total loyalty on the voyage. The first mate had taken care of provisions being brought aboard. The captain glanced over the inventory lists. He questioned the first mate on only two items: 150

gallons of whiskey, at $1.25 per gallon, and 20 gallons of whiskey, at 80 cents per gallon. Everyone knew exactly who would be drinking the expensive whiskey and who would be drinking the cheaper swill. The expensive whiskey was designated for the experienced crewmembers that specialized in artillery, the Dahlgrens, to be exact. The ship's safety and survival depended on these experienced artillerymen, these men that had years of experience in the operation and firing of the Dahlgrens. These men could knock a sparrow's eye out at 5,000 feet with those Dahlgrens. These artillerymen had been the saviors of the American Union Army on land and at sea. Two were commissioned lieutenants when they were mustered out of military service.

Of course, the Holm family didn't know any of this when they finally decided on this particular ship. They decided on the ship, not for its appearance or stature, not for its sails that lay asleep while it was docked, but its departure date and time. Father was told they would leave at high tide. After hearing the departure time, Father hurried back to the Göteborg marketplace to sell the oxen and cart. Along the way, his eyes widened to see old soaks loosening their purse strings to the harlots' painted faces and succumbing to persuasive harlotry. Receiving what he considered a fair price, he walked back to the ship and paid the fare of passage for two adults and two children.

captain pered?
Lieutenant 7th ?
warden ?

records ?

CHAPTER SIXTEEN

The family had purchased fifteen loaves of Swedish rye along with a dozen loaves of limpa bread to carry on board. They also had their seed potatoes and pickled pike. The captain hollered down to them as they struggled with the barrels on the gangplank, "Stop right there!" Father panicked and froze in fear that the ship's officers had changed their minds and wouldn't allow them aboard the ship. Beads of perspiration ran down Father's face and off the end of his nose like a hard rain. Again, the captain hollered, "Wait, and let me get you some help with those barrels." The captain came down from the deck and introduced himself to Father and Mother. He explained that he was in sole command and that if they needed anything, to let the lieutenant know. This was out of character for a man that held a deep contempt for immigrants. In actuality he was only trying to frighten the Holms, which he succeeded in doing with his gritty profanity.

That night the whole crew got a little tipsy from their whiskey ration, but that was to be expected and quite normal before casting off for months. The captain wrote in his journal, "These peasants that have signed aboard can mostly only sign with their mark or X. They are miserably poor souls, illiterate, and it seems from a distance, quite lazy. You can't stand downwind from them as they have a deplorable odor about them, but I find qualities that could be admired. They are polite, overly friendly, and gracious. They look like they live in harmony amongst themselves."

One could believe from the quote in the captain's journal that he did have a strong prejudice against the immigrants. Possibly from his childhood, he believed that an occupation that didn't involve the sea was degrading, especially an occupation that involved cultivation. The captain had little respect for anyone that hunted game or trapped animals for a living. He found the notion to be disgusting, primitive, and quite inhumane. The captain held no respect for men that used such means for providing for their families. The captain was a true hypocrite in every sense of the word.

The moon was high and full that night and some of the passengers were on deck milling about. They had been boarding the ship for hours over on the starboard side and were filing up the two gangplanks, single file. Many of the passengers were so drunk that they clung to the manropes with both hands trying to keep their balance without plunging into the harbor. So many had worried themselves half to death about the voyage that they had sat in pubs or saloons along the docks for days. One woman was breastfeeding her newborn daughter as she slowly walked up the gangplank. Sailors up above on the deck whistled and heckled the poor woman the whole time she was nursing. She finally made it into the ship and out of the sight of the leering sailors.

It always seemed like the harbor rats knew exactly which ships to board and which ships not to board. It was a seaman's superstition that if rats came on board, it would be a safe trip. Erick had nothing else to do so he watched and counted all the rats boarding.

Erick watched the rats running up the ropes faster than the passengers could board. No one ever knew if they were running to the food in the galley or to the whiskey barrels, but the rats were always first on board and first to pick their cruise accommodations. Those rats ran back and forth from bow to stern, helter-skelter over passengers, farm animals, and tied down freight. The crew could be seen watching the rats running up the riggings. They were taking bets on which were the thinnest, fattest, slowest, and fastest. The crew knew it would be a safe voyage and welcomed the rats with open arms. The sailors would joke, "Every second rat gets the cheese," and lick their lips in laughter. They also knew that if the rats ran down the riggings and off the ship, the ship would be doomed.

As the ship was about to cast off, harmonicas, fiddles, guitars, and the like could be heard all across the ship. It didn't matter what type of misfortune these immigrants were leaving behind, they all had glamorous dreams of the New World and a better life.

Chapter Seventeen

The ship left the Göteborg harbor late Saturday night with a high tide. The heat from the furnaces made it so hot down in the passenger's compartments that the immigrants were shedding their clothes like snakes in a pit. Out past the harbor in the cool sea breeze, with the sounds of the break-water behind them, the captain abruptly shut the furnaces off which had only been used to get the ship out of the harbor and into the wind. The heat in the coal holds dissipated quickly and the immigrants' clothing went right back on. The cold from the sea rapidly came through the oak planks and it wasn't long until a deep cold gripped the bowels of the ship.

Sunday morning came like every other Sunday before. Lutheran church services were held on the ship, the same as on land. For Swedish, Danish, Finnish, and Norwegian scriptures were of Christian denomination. Those that wanted to attend did so, and those uninterested stayed down in the holds. After leaving Göteborg, the next cargoes of immigrants were picked up in Helsinki, Hanko and then Turku, Finland, and then the ship traveled across the Baltic to Stockholm. From there, they sailed down around southern Sweden and to Copenhagen, Denmark, up north to Halmsted and Varberg, Sweden. They were now passing

Göteborg again, which was their origin. They then crossed the North Sea, picking up passengers from Hull and Leeds, England. At that time, Göteborg was the second most populous city in all of Scandinavia just because that was the city from which most of the immigrants made their exodus. Ship captains were overwhelmed by the monumental numbers of people waiting for transportation at each dockside, despite the stories circulating of atrocities and all the sickness and death on the transports. Cholera, tuberculosis, and the plague were epidemic during this time.

Weeks into the voyage, down in the freezing coal holds, the terror in the eyes of those poor souls would soon be labeled as hunger, malnutrition, and starvation. The years of famine and drought had taken their toll on the poor Swedes. The potato famine years had overtaken the Swedish countryside. Lack of food had forced tens of thousands to take refuge in the New World. Crop failures had accelerated the flow of immigrants. In many cases, these immigrants were following relatives that had gone before them. They were headed mainly toward the undeveloped farmlands of the Midwest of North America, mainly in Minnesota, Illinois, and Wisconsin. America represented their hope for prosperity.

The Holms were indeed sodbusters, leaving the only place they knew, where the dream had died, and heading for unspoiled territory in which to begin anew. Not being able to speak English did not slow them down. Like them, most of the passengers were young and dirt poor with young children of their own. Erick and little Charles were two of the possibly more than two hundred children aboard the ship. Father complained about the accommodations numerous times and finally the captain sent a crewmember down to have their accommodations changed. The sailor was known as a "powder monkey," and was half drunk and laughing. He said his name was Sven and that he was from Stockholm originally. Father whispered to Mother that he didn't believe this man called Sven and didn't think that was his real name.

Sven led the Holms past cavernous areas and down a rickety dark stairwell. Sven spoke Swedish so it was easy to follow his directions. They walked down another set of stairwells, and with each stairwell it got darker and darker and now it was harder to follow Sven.

"This is it," Sven said as he stopped dead in his tracks.

"Where, what is this?" Father exclaimed.

Sven told Father, "You can pick anyplace you want down here, Captain says." And with that, he walked away into the darkness laughing hysterically. It seems that Father had complained once too often to this captain who found farmers, hunters, and trappers to be the lowest form of humanity.

Once situated in the lower coal holds, everything began to disintegrate for the family, both physically and mentally. As Father told the family, "This is like being in the belly of a whale, intestines and all." The family found out in a very short time that they were located in a forward hold. It was in the bow section and next to the steam furnaces. It would have been nice to ring for room service and have dinner delivered, but not on this trip. It would also have been nice to have their own bath and stateroom, but those hadn't been invented as yet on ships of the period.

There was a smorgasbord of Viking descendents from Finland, Denmark, and Sweden, and a few Norwegian families that had slipped aboard. First these Norsemen, Swedes, and Finlanders hated each other to a point where a simple misunderstanding due to differences in cultures soon turned into fistfights over virtually nothing. When the fight would end, no one could remember what the fight was about.

In addition to being packed into the coal holds, one had to put up with his neighbor's lack of personal hygiene, as it had been months in most cases since anyone had bathed. It took days to adjust to the foul smells that nearly buckled Erick's knees the first days down in the holds. It never dawned on Erick that some of the smell actually came from him. Erick was mortified by the ongoing hygiene problem. His stomach felt like a wet sock being turned inside out. The North Atlantic was leaking in almost everywhere between the giant oak planks. The holds were wet, damp, and stunk to high heaven. There were no windows to see out of or from which to breathe clean fresh ocean air. There were no windows at all in this giant wooden coffin, only the windows in your mind.

"Oh, if the captain would only fire up the furnaces again," thought Erick. Coming out of Göteborg harbor, passengers had complained bitterly of the oppressive heat and noise from the furnaces, but everyone would love to have that heat and noise right now.

With the full North Atlantic to the west, calm had been replaced by fear of the unknown. These immigrants, who were, after all, only landlubbers, began to come apart at the seams much like the ship itself. These farmers, foresters, and trappers were completely out of their element. These hardened Scandinavians loved their beloved homeland, with its wide open spaces, blue skies, twinkling stars, crystal clear lakes, and sunshine. All those things were now only pleasant memories. They were locked in this deep black hole, down in the belly of the whale. It did not take long until the smooth, even sounds of the bow cutting through ten foot waves was replaced by the bow crashing rhythmically, headlong into twenty-foot waves. This was the sailing season!

Up above on deck, you could hear cargo that was not securely tied down crashing from one end of the ship to the other. Crewmembers were screaming out orders to one another, but these hardened Scandinavian Vikings below deck couldn't distinguish what was being said, since they couldn't speak or understand the English language. Down in the coal holds, men, women, children, and farm animals were screaming and crying as they were hurled from one oak plank to another.

Erick noticed his father's eyes watering, his nostrils twitching, and a deep redness spreading across his face. Suddenly it dawned on Erick that Father was afraid to cry for fear that he would make his family cry. All Father's grumbling, grouching, snits, and stews were mere camouflage for a deep sensitive heart that only God could reveal.

There were no ways to safely stay in place. They had no ropes to tie themselves down, so they were all left to the mercy of the North Atlantic. They tried holding onto one another, but continued to bounce around the coal holds like little rubber balls.

CHAPTER EIGHTEEN

Erick asked his father where they were that it had turned so terribly cold. The family could no longer keep their feet on the ship's oak planks due to the cold penetrating through. Whatever they could find, they placed between the planks and themselves. Only the captain knew precisely where the ship had been blown and exactly how far off course they had become. The Holms only knew that they had been in a ferocious storm for close to five days. What they didn't know was that the ship had held a course of sixty degrees latitude, which ran parallel through Stockholm, Sweden. A straight line between Stockholm and New York City had originally been the captain's course before the storm. New York was approximately forty degrees latitude. The storm had taken the ship north to within seven hundred miles off the southern tip of Greenland and was skirting the Labrador Sea. Only the captain knew they were fifty-five degrees latitude and forty degrees longitude. That combination placed them precisely one thousand miles east of Labrador.

To ease the pain of the twenty-five foot waves on his beaten and bruised ship, the captain had deliberately turned the ship north and had most possibly prevented the ship from ending up in Davy Jones' Locker. The Holm family didn't know that their captain, with his experience as captain of the

Monitor and this fine ship, had in fact saved their lives. By turning the ship away from the storm, the captain had saved the ship from violently coming apart, sinking, and all aboard being lost as so many other ships had done in the North Atlantic. The captain knew the storm had added another five or six days, even a week, onto the voyage.

Many concerns had to be dealt with because of their new course. First and foremost were icebergs. Immediately, he put the crew on watch, not only to watch for icebergs but also to watch each other in case one should nod off. It was so cold that the crewmembers were put on short watches of only an hour. Each crewmember realized the seriousness and impending danger of their situation. To keep lookouts alert, the captain offered a prize of ten pounds of tobacco to whoever saw the first iceberg. They had come to the rescue in dramatic style. It was almost unheard of in naval circles, but the crew had stopped drinking whiskey in order to keep their minds clear due to the iceberg danger. Another concern was food, or shortage of food. Additionally, there was the concern for the health of all the passengers down in the coal holds. The captain knew they were freezing and that the passenger deaths would become more frequent, adding up to possibly several deaths every day they were at sea. As a naval officer commanding a ship, his first obligation was, of course, the ship. The second was his officers and crew. Lastly were the uneducated and illegal immigrants to whom he had given no guarantees of safety, arrival date, or course of travel. The captain had already saved the ship from coming apart and slipping away under the brutal North Atlantic. The captain's decision to stay the course and not turn south would turn out to be prudent on the captain's part. The lives of the immigrants could not take precedence over anything else. The immigrants were expendable; the ship wasn't.

The ship had settled down to the steady routine of clear water sailing. There were no icebergs, no whales, and only occasionally a school of dolphins. It became a little colder each day, but the sun did shine down on the ice-covered deck from time to time. There had been no cleaning of the deck by the crew now for days due to the sheet of clear ice that prevented any such cleaning routine. Rather than the daily ritual of deck maintenance, the crew spent extra hours cleaning their berths in the forecastle.

All the crewmembers slept in a somewhat confined area in hammocks hung one on top of the other like bunk beds. They were made with heavy seamen's hemp and swung freely with the rising and falling of the bow cutting steadily through the waves. All hands would be piped to breakfast and dinner, two meals a day provided that weather conditions permitted. Daily Dahlgren exercises were held by the artillerymen and powder monkeys until the decks became unsafe for the exercises due to ice. The topsails were forever being resewn because of the continuous wind damage they sustained twenty-four hours a day. Crewmembers tried to maintain and beautify the ship by cleaning the brass with brick dust and brine. Their duties were maintained despite the weather. Many days went without the crew being piped to dinner or breakfast due to the fierce weather conditions. Crewmembers were piped to lunch on occasion when dinner and breakfast had both been missed. The artillerymen had no time or days off, even if the weather was impossible up on deck. The crew may have missed breakfast, lunch, and dinner but the distribution of whiskey rations by the master's mate went on without regard to weather. Breakfast was eight bells and dinner was six bells, followed by quarters at nine bells.

The foremast hands were commonly rough, tarpaulin-hatted, tobacco chewers, long-soured scoundrels in love with their mistress, the ship. After a ration of the better whiskey, the artillerymen would talk with foolish smiles lighting up their hard-wrinkled seamen faces. The ship would clear for action when the artillerymen readied their Dahlgrens for fighting practice. These men worked together like a well-oiled machine. They specialized in what they did and they did it well. They enjoyed their competence, companionship, and the small pleasures of life, and suffered only occasionally from boredom. The crew would raffle with coppers for tobacco while telling lewd jokes and stories; "a motley crew they were." Christian immigrants were offended to see sailors gambling.

Their spirits would rise high at nine bells, which was when the master's mate distributed their share, the better share, of the two whiskeys on board. The ship was a semi-man-of-war, but to these artillerymen, she was their mistress, and they would sail with all reasonable sail aboard as long as there was a steady wind coming in over her larboard quarter. When the seas were sharp, she would throw a fine sheet of spray to leeward with each even-measured pitch. At the times of Dahlgren gun practice, there was a generally diffused happiness and a discreet wave of mirth and satisfaction that rippled over the forecastle. Ten knots was greeted during gun practice with thrumping on the deck. The enthusiasm was sufficient that the officer of the watch told the mate of the watch, "Attend to all that trampling and bellowing. They sound like a herd of drunken heifers in love with the bull."

The captain spoke in a less harsh manner to his ship's boy, who tried to remain dutiful at all times to his captain. The boy was Erick's age and had a blissful ignorance about him. Unlike the crew, the captain would never rail or bellow against his cabin boy. Some said the captain treated the boy as his own son.

Bib ship inspection regulation?

CHAPTER NINETEEN

They were totally in God's hands now, and the terrified immigrants knew just that. Mothers held onto their babies as if on a roller coaster, squeezing them closely for dear life. Families tried to hold onto one another to keep from being thrown against the inner oak beams of the beast. Deep cuts and heavy bleeding were common, along with broken arms and legs. It was impossible to keep from bringing everything in their stomachs up and over everyone and everything. Human vomit, it seemed, covered every square inch of their living space.

Human suffering was only increased by the fact that, along with these poor souls, there were also their animals. In addition to the fare paid by the family, Father had to pay for each animal he brought on board. Father had bought two goats for milking and a dozen chickens for eating from the Göteborg market. He hadn't understood when he paid the fare that the animals would be sharing their living quarters side by side with them. Within minutes, the family realized the magnitude of the problem of togetherness. It only took seconds for the animals to develop seasickness, and it seemed as if they all lost control of their bodily functions immediately.

All human and animal waste had to be dealt with, and the ship's crew had prepared for these necessities. The ship's fare included half barrels with ropes and small coal shovels. It didn't take but a very short amount of time for the waste to grow enormous in volume. Passengers used the shovels to scoop the waste into the half barrels. This was then followed by lifting the half barrels, one step at a time, up the stairwells to the deck. At first, volunteers were impossible to come by, but then everybody was volunteering. The immigrants would almost come to blows over this chore, all trying to get up on deck to the clean fresh air. Once on deck, the gut-wrenching, hard vomiting of so many older passengers, both men and women, led to numerous cases of vomiting blood. This bodily function forced their false teeth right out and over the deck railings, gone to the depths of the Atlantic, and Davy Jones' Locker, for eternity.

It seemed like forever until the ship finally calmed down and that was only after the captain had changed direction and followed his new course southward. He was far from the prime meridian, but the ship was in reasonably good shape for its age and nautical miles. She was frightening to look at, but her sails had held, and she hadn't hit an iceberg. The ship had been blown hundreds of miles north from her original course. The whole ship had become terribly cold and the immigrants begged for the captain to turn the steam furnaces back on, but their pleading fell on deaf ears as usual. It was so cold down in the bowels of the coal holds that if a man had to go in one of the buckets, his penis could freeze if he didn't act quickly. Father said in all of his years, he had never been as cold as he was in that coal hold. Without a fire to keep from freezing, the only solution was to huddle together for warmth.

Erick's clothing was made primarily from elk skins. This was a plus when it came to keeping warm. Even his shirt was made from elk skins. With such extreme cold down in the holds, one might think that it would have induced the captain to turn on the steam furnaces, but it wasn't to be. The immigrants were now officially in a state of semi-hibernation, barely able to walk around due to the cold. Men had become lazy and sometimes refused to take part in hauling the waste and seawater combination they had collected in the half barrels up the ladders. By not moving around they somehow claimed that they were warm and comfortable. It seemed like the women were doing all the waste hauling.

Some men went up to ask the first mate if they could help work around the ship, just so they could stay warm. Always answering in his usual way, the first mate bellowed, "No!" None dared to stand up to the first mate for fear that he would have the crew throw anyone overboard who dared question him.

The first mate stood on deck like a tall oak in the forest. His massive shoulders exposed his powerful chest and arms, and he had hands like a giant. No one on board was going to contradict this man. The crew and officers always seemed to be busy doing one kind of work or another. The first mate and captain knew that an idle crewmember was a bored crewmember. Bored crewmembers led to bad tempers and temper flare-ups, which soon led to fistfights and knives being pulled; so discipline was the rule. The greenies were not skilled seamen as yet, but they jumped to a task when an order was given and made few mistakes. There was a rapid transformation of the greenhorns into sailors. After a time at sea, they hardly knew themselves as the clumsy clodhoppers they at first appeared to be.

It was not long until the first signs of the bitter cold in the holds developed into a medical disaster. The mix of seawater and urine on the hold floor had led to the rotting of everyone's boots and shoes. Evidence of this could be seen by the number of individuals laid up with cut and bleeding feet. Their boots and shoes had decayed and had become only shredded pieces of hides, held tight to blistered and bleeding toes. Their clothing had been found to be horribly inadequate for such a harsh voyage.

Sometimes at night, to break up the monotony and misery, music could be heard throughout the ship. One man had a fiddle, another a sounding horn, and yet a third had a tambourine. This little bit of gaiety seemed to liven up the residents of the holds. Erick wishfully thought, "Oh, how wonderful it would be to have a hot steaming cup of coffee."

All types of trading went on down in the hold by the sixth week on the ship. Some individuals actually turned to communal life. Father, to his dismay, witnessed the unthinkable. A young man, desperate for a blanket or two, offered the sexual services of his wife up for trade. Finally, the young man found a taker for the trade. The wife soon appeared naked as a jaybird. The wife led a man by the hand off to a somewhat secluded area in the hold, they took care of business, and the trade was consummated. The husband got his blanket, then the wife and husband huddled beneath the blanket so she could get her clothes back on and life in the coal hold went on.

One day, Mother was asked to assist with a child birthing. She had no experience as a doctor or as a midwife, but no one else volunteered to help. The woman said it was her first child. After many hours of painfully violent and tedious labor, she bore a baby girl that she named Anna after Erick's mother. The baby was healthy and active. Now the sounds of a hungry baby echoed through the coal holds.

Word spread like a firestorm about Mother's birthing the baby. It wasn't long before Mother had another patient. After a cursory examination, Mother found the woman to be extremely ill with a high fever, a scarcely perceptible pulse, irregular breathing, and alarming twitching. The woman hadn't eaten in a number of days and was completely dehydrated. Mother gave her some of the food she had been hoarding and kept her where she could be cared for. A few days later the woman had beaten the fever and was well enough to go back with her family.

Because of her success with healing, Mother couldn't get any rest. It got to be that Mother was known down in the coal holds as Doc Holm. Another young woman brought her son to Mother to look at. The little boy was about the same age as little Charles. He had an abscess on his back, which Mother cured. Another child was brought to her that had frozen feet. Mother soaked the boy's feet in cold water. It worked well, and the boy was all right. There were frequent cases of frostbitten toes. One particular case was a teenage boy whose toes had been frozen for weeks. By the time he came to Mother, the toes were too far gone. Mother had to cut the blackened toes off, cutting loose the dead tissue and joints, and severing the tendons. That was the first time Father's skinning knife was used on the ship for something other than cutting loaves of bread. It took four grown men to hold that boy down while Mother cut and sawed until the toes fell to the oak floor. Mother saved that boy's life.

The predominant medical problem on board was syphilis. Nearly every crewmember suffered from the disease. The captain knew this would be a problem and was prepared to head it off. The first mate had each crewmember digest mercury in the form of a pill. The name for the pill was calomel. The side effects could be dangerous. The phrase, "mad as a hatter," was a reference to hat makers who used mercury in the process of hat making. They would become crazy from breathing in the fumes.

Awakened sometime in the night by the violent pitching of the ship, passengers became uneasy and knew that the ship was once again in a desperate fight for survival. They knew this storm must be a real nor'easter, the type of storm everyone had been dreading since leaving Sweden.

There were no doctors, nurses, or medical staff on board. Broken limbs were commonplace among the passengers from being tossed back and forth. Broken bones would be splinted together with whatever could be found. Open cuts, both shallow and deep, were stitched back together by Norwegian and Swedish fishermen, using fishing line they had brought to use in North America.

Each family was allowed up on the deck each day for a few minutes, providing the weather conditions were conducive to safety. They would stretch their bodies, and at the same time, relieve themselves over the side if at all possible.

When the sea would calm to some degree, the captain would drop the sails to slow the ship. This would be followed by the crewmembers fishing alongside the experienced Scandinavian fishermen. They would fish for whatever they could catch. For the most part, they caught North Sea cod. This was not only filling, but also a delectable treat on everyone's tongues. When fishing was good the steaming, clattery, pungent copper kitchen was packed with smiling, happy volunteers preparing the delicacy in the heart of the ship. Sometimes hundreds of cod would be caught, cleaned, and cooked on the giant wood cookstoves. Platters of stupendous, succulent cod were piled high for the not-so-picky, hungry, and nearly starved passengers. Since there was no way to divide up the cod equally, it became every man, women, and child for themselves. There were no clean white aprons, tied neatly with prim and proper bows for serving, no silver utensils, or linen napkins. Instead, there were only greasy, busy fingers moving rapidly so as not to miss a single scrap of cod. Fingers were licked sparkly clean so as to savor every delicate morsel.

Some passengers hoarded the fish, taking far more than they could ever consume and leaving others with virtually nothing to eat. Verbal bantering was always followed by loud disagreements, which often led to pushing, shoving, and heated arguing.

Erick peered through the busy kitchen doorway. With his lips quivering and his taste buds aflutter, he was so close to the heavenly fried cod and yet so far. He continued to watch the whole operation of frying cod, which brought back instant memories of Mother frying up pike in their little cabin home in Lotorp. A tear welled up in Erick's eye and hung heavily for the longest time until falling to his cheek and rolling like a snowball down onto his shirt. He was pushed violently out of the doorway and told, "Move out of the way, boy."

Surely there is nothing as evocative as smell to spur the memory and so Erick stood crunched against the doorframe and kitchen wall. He reached out and pleaded for but a piece of the delicious smell. Erick could only stand by as a spectator, watching total strangers devour hoards of whatever they could get their hands on. This was truly an education on ignorance, rudeness, and etiquette for this poor little immigrant boy.

There was, of course, the unwritten law of the sea, that the captain, officers, and crew received their food first. The crew had a somewhat balanced diet. They each had a ration of a hominy concoction and lard on one day, salt pork and flour the next, and cornmeal along with pork the following day. Ground corn and flour were mixed with fish that had been salted in barrels. Fresh loaves of bread were baked daily on the wood-burning stoves. If there were potatoes to go with the meal, the crew devoured them quickly without any forethought of leaving anything for their passengers, who were already suffering from dysentery, ulcers, and boils.

There were no extra potatoes to feed the hundreds of passengers. At least on these fishing ventures, each and every passenger ate, even if they only received very little. Most families had purchased loaves of potato bread at the Göteborg market, so they at least had bread to go along with their cod meal. Those that had brought bread, potatoes, carrots, and hardtack guarded it like they had bars of gold. No one could be trusted to be respectful of another's food, animals, belongings, or even wives.

When fishing would conclude, sails would be raised, and the captain and crew would return to the business of running the ship. Families were herded back down the slippery dark stairwells to their waiting coal holds. With no ice or refrigeration, all the fish had to be eaten right then and there. If any was not eaten it was fed to the animals below deck to help keep them healthy. The whole ship seemed to be covered with cod entrails and scales. All the heads and organs from cleaning hundreds of fish at one time seemed impossible to remove. Buckets on ropes were lowered over the sides to gather seawater for swabbing the deck. The deck had to be cleared of fish scales before the crew could tend to the process of running the ship.

The weather improved to a degree and strong winds filled the sails. This graceful swan cruised at a fast rate of possibly ten knots. This allowed much of the crashing of the bow to subside. Passengers became more at ease, now actually forcing temporary smiles and joking amongst each other. The worst was over, so they thought.

Days passed that turned into weeks. Now it seemed as if a cold ice had fallen over the ship. The ship leaked at every seam, reducing their sparse accommodations to a soaking, sodden, and stinking rat hole. Mother wrapped the children's feet with blanket strips, since their boots were entirely useless. Reluctant to venture forward up the stairwells to toilets, they turned the bilges into their personal toilets, which became stagnant and foul. Passengers, including the Holms, were driven out from the coal holds many times by voracious cockroaches that ate leather and skin from their feet while they were asleep and even drank ink wells dry in the officer's quarters.

The sickness all started with a few passengers sneezing and coughing. It quickly spread, leading to hundreds becoming deathly ill. A sudden hush fell over the coal holds as the first child died. Both of the parents cried for hours, still holding the cold, stiff, blue child in their collective arms. It didn't take long for crewmembers to clamber down the stairwells. A few of the crewmembers forcibly tore the dead child from its mother's loving arms and one threw the child over his broad shoulders. He then scurried up the stairwell with the mother and father close behind screaming. After a quick service of less than a dozen words, the child was committed to the sea by means of a wooden slide. She was gently slid down into the cold Atlantic, and so it was again and again and again for every death after that.

The crewmembers had to move quickly after each death in order to prevent the plague. The plague was an epidemic disease that caused a high rate of mortality. In the 1880s, the plague was known to wipe out whole villages within days of discovery. As each day at sea elapsed, more and more immigrants died.

Father came back down the stairwell after emptying two half barrels up and over the railings. He passed a young mother that had died hours before as she attempted to feed her grayish blue premature baby girl. She must have bled to death, as there was a tremendous amount of blood surrounding her. She just sat there with her back leaning up against the coal hold beams, as if waiting to change the baby's diaper.

After someone would die, especially the older family members, the family seemed to care about the person in ways they should have while they were still alive. These desperate souls were deprived of all humanity and exposed to inhumane, nightmarish conditions, twenty-four hours a day. One couldn't cough without six immigrants nearby catching pneumonia.

Newly formed neighbors and families huddled together for warmth. The immigrants could all see their breath down in the holds. Those holds had gotten colder than even the crew could have imagined, colder than a witch's tit. Now it became an effort to go up on deck. Water on the wooden deck had turned to an icy slush that only added to the misery. Passengers asked the first mate if he would turn on the steam furnaces to provide desperately needed heat, but it couldn't be done, because the precious coal was in short supply. He told the passengers that the coal was needed further into the voyage once they reached North America.

Brutal howling winds whistled through the coal holds. The ship leaped and lurched in what were now forty-foot swells, with the second mate, taking a trick at the wheel, with a grit and bravado. The winds were clocked at seventy knots. The sea could swallow up the ship in one frothy gulp. Ice had formed three inches thick on the deck, wheelhouse, and railings. The captain sent men up on deck wearing the type of spiked boots that lumberjacks wore. The men each carried double-sided axes. They tried to chop the ice loose from the wheelhouse, deck, and stairwell to the wheelhouse. The captain had become a prisoner, locked in the wheelhouse like a giant coffin.

The captain was up in the wheelhouse, his eyes, still glazed over from his nightly rum dinner, transfixed on the towering waves. Waves pounded over the starboard side and crashed against the rattling wheelhouse windows. Several crew members burst into the cabin, with wind and waves following them right through the door. A fireman's assistant shakily told the captain that he thought the ship was being swallowed up by an angry sea god. The captain remained as steadfast as a rock, holding the wheel tightly in his callused hands. Staring straight ahead, the captain began to tell one of his stories as he retightened the cap of his rum flask. It was a story that was told to him by his father and his father before him—the legendary story of the "Finnish Ship."

Just then a wave crashed through the windows on the starboard side. Wind, waves, and broken glass only added to the drama of the captain's story, and they all prepared to meet their angry god. The captain told of a ship sent from Sweden, loaded almost entirely with Finnish passengers, who had been sent to settle the land in America. When they came closer to the American continent, the vessel began leaking from a nor'easter. The crew pumped sea water for three days. Try as they might, the water finally got the better of them and the damage was irreparable. Besides the crew, there were three hundred Finns onboard. When the crew saw that all hope of saving the ship was gone, they jumped into the lifeboats under the pretext of investigating the leak. In reality, they were saving their own lives. One of the Finns, by the name of Lickoven, noticed the crew escaping and jumped into the lifeboat himself. The ship sank like a stone with all passengers.

Those in lifeboats did reach the shores of New England. This ship was called "Det Finske Skepper," (the legendary "Finnish Ship"). The ship's doctor had been ordered by the captain to board the lifeboats, but he promptly refused to leave his people and stayed with the vessel, parishing with the rest. Other ships carring Finnish passengers that never reached their intended American destinations were: the *Purmerlander,* the *Kerck,* the *Vergulde Arent,* the *St. Jacob,* and the *Waghen.*

The captain was worried more about the weight of the building thickness of the ice than becoming free. Now the sea was taking control of his ship and tossing it about like a cork. He had to turn the furnaces on to create enough power to keep the ship steady and to stop the continued growth of the heavy ice. If he could get out of the storm alive, he would worry about coal later at a village where he could replenish his supply. The captain had the crew go up to chop ice in three-hour shifts. Because of the terrific danger, each man had to tie himself on to something before even beginning to swing his ax. It took thirty hours to free the captain from the wheelhouse alone.

Each wave that the ship's bow struck sent a shudder throughout the ship. It sounded like the ship would break into pieces and dive effortlessly down to Davy Jones' Locker with all hands and passengers lost. That would have been the story if not for the captain's steering straight into the wind and waves under full steam. After a week of plunging through heavy, packed ice that would have punctured any other vessel then afloat, the ship broke clear into open water.

The illegal immigrants' accommodations were in direct opposition to the luxury of the captain's quarters. The aft cabins of eighteenth century sailing ships were the noblest interior spaces ever created by shipbuilders. Airy and light, these were no dingy, blocky, cubed compartments. They were full of subtle curves from the tumble home of topsides, which was a seaman's description of elegance and spaciousness one had never seen before. The captain's quarters were topside, directly below deck, with windows stretched across the stern from port to starboard. Camber of beams and deck were dappled with water-reflected light bouncing through the curved windows of the stern. These were the captain's quarters where he could walk out onto the balustraded stern gallery, sniff the ocean breeze, and contemplate the bubbling wake tumbling below him. He could lounge about with a glass of his favorite rum and take his mind off the poor withering souls below in the coal holds.

Much of the Holms' food that they had hoarded for over a month had gone rancid to the point that the community of rats even turned their noses up at the smell of it. Now they had the added job of hauling pickled pike up the stairwell in buckets and pitching all their pike into the sea. The Holms were in disbelief that after hauling the pike all across Sweden by wagon, up onto the ship, and down into the coal hold, that they now had to pitch it all over the side.

CHAPTER TWENTY

The plight of these wretched souls was only exacerbated by their chronic medical problems. Chronic headaches were epidemic amongst the immigrant women, who also complained of such symptoms as general weakness or stomach discomfort. Numerous women had violent spasms and couldn't take food or drink any longer. Women and children deteriorated rapidly from drinking and eating almost nothing, and then they began to suffer from partial paralysis, impaired eyesight, spinal pain, and hemorrhaging lungs. Those who were part of the vibrant spiritualist movement of the period probably kept alive and well longer than others. Many immigrants became claustrophobic from being imprisoned for weeks down in the holds. Families quarreled amongst each other and the family quarrels spilled over to quarrels with their neighbors.

Anna Holm rose above the uneducated farming limitations of her time. She was intelligent, sheltered, naive, and impressionable all rolled into one young woman. During these harsh, hard weeks, she felt, although only temporarily, that she had been victimized by the man she loved and trusted. Anna had a clean, warm home with toilet facilities, privacy, neighbors, and church. She had a soft, warm bed and a roaring fireplace. She had to give all of this up, only for it to be replaced by death and animal waste. There were times that she had symptoms of hysteria, which was held to be a female ailment of the time.

Death and dying spread from hold to hold and deck to deck. Death spared no one. No distinction to nation or origin was made when death came knocking at the door. Illness, dying, and death became as sure as the sun coming up in the east and going down in west. Families waited in their prisons for the eventual knock on their doors from Mr. Death.

With death and dying going on all around the ship, Erick closed his eyes and thought back to his hunting and trapping days on Potato Creek. He thought of the Namekagan men lying in wait for him and how he felt they were out to kill him in one way or another. He thought out loud, "Could the Namekagan men have deliberately spared my life back in the Lotorp Woods, just to have me die here?" Erick's thoughts were broken by the wailing of yet another young woman whose baby had just died.

As spring approached, the winds seemed to increase, the waves grew higher and higher, and the swells deeper and deeper. Snow began to fall, slowly at first, but then it increased in velocity. It did not take long before the snow became measurable on the deck, which was already coated with a sheet of ice. A crewmember was always assigned to iceberg watch since the ship was crossing the North Atlantic Ocean. No icebergs were seen through the heavy snow. Snow was coating the sails. To prevent them from being damaged, the captain ordered them lowered. The seas became quite calm in the torrential snow. This gave the crew a chance to slow down. Now the ship seemed to bob like a cork in the gentle swells.

A thunderous roar from behind the heavily falling snow suddenly broke the quiet solitude. Water sprayed up on the deck, covering members of the crew that had been lowering the sails. Everyone on deck turned toward the thunderous sound. It was a high-pitched resonance, an ear-splitting sound. Several of the crew held their hands up to cover their ears. An instant later, the clear aroma of gunpowder settled over the ship's deck.

The first mate was below deck enjoying a cup of coffee when he heard the sounds above. He flew up the stairwell, three steps at a time, reaching the deck in time to see in the distance through the blizzard-like snow, a set of sails. The captain raised his spyglass up to his eyes, concentrating as best he could in the heat of the moment. He focused the lens on the full white sails in the distance. He bellowed the words, "Pirates!" There is nothing so electrifying as that cry from a captain. They must have been following the ship and when the sails dropped, they knew the ship was vulnerable.

The first mate was by now alongside the captain. With a firm command, the captain barked, "Unlatch the Dahlgren cannons, load, and prepare to fire." The powder monkeys scrambled to remove the heavy canvas covers from the Dahlgrens and proceeded to pivot them into battle positions. They rolled easily down the brass rails and were locked down into firing position in a moment. Brass sights were leveled.

The pirate ship was slightly to the south, so the captain had the ship turned. Now the Dahlgrens faced the pirate ship. Each crew chief waited for the first mate's order to fire. The snow was coming down so heavily now that all that was visible of the pirate ship were her topsails and masts. Without hesitation the order was given, "Fire!"

The Dahlgrens exploded in unison and their power pushed them back up the full length of the brass rails. The whole ship shuddered; smoke covered the deck from one end to the other. It took on the look of a foggy graveyard.

Before the shells could even land, orders to reload were heard. The shells all fell short of the pirate ship, falling harmlessly into the sea, barely creating the sound of a splash behind the fog bank. Both the captain and lieutenant began to curse the crew chiefs, with unbridled profanity, for their failure to hit their designated targets, which were the masts and sails.

The eleven-inch Dahlgrens were re-aimed toward the upper masts as the lieutenant had ordered, followed by his order to fire. The Dahlgrens exploded and rocked back on their rails. The captain watched through his spyglass and was witness to two of the pirate ship's masts crashing down through the sails, and then down onto the deck below. Again, the lieutenant screamed his demands to the crew chiefs and powder monkeys to load and fire at the remaining mast peering up through the fog. The four Dahlgrens barked, covering the artillerymen with a thick coating of spent gunpowder. All their faces were now blackened and their hair bristled as if frozen in place.

The captain raised his spyglass toward the remaining mast. A smile crept across his face as the last remaining mast disappeared from view. He never wavered. He burst forth with a further command to aim at their wheelhouse. The wheelhouse was the pirate ship's command center and most likely held whoever was in charge of their ship.

The order to fire was given and the Dahlgrens exploded, first, second, and third in the line, followed by the deck cannon. Total silence followed and then they heard the crushing sounds of lead contacting oak. The fog was too thick to determine what had been hit. The artillerymen swabbed each of the Dahlgrens barrels tenderly as if they were caressing their women. All four were clean, unobstructed, and ready within minutes. They were all quickly reloaded, aimed, and directed toward what had now become a ghostly image of a ship of broken masts partially seen through the thick fog. Once again the lieutenant commanded the chiefs, in full rhythmic profanity, to try and knock out the wheelhouse, but the artillerymen could barely see a sliver of the ship's silhouette.

"Fire at will!" he bellowed. It was clear to everyone on deck that the captain had become obsessed with halting the pirate ship and would simply let it drift aimlessly forever at sea. He was boiling mad and was taking his anger out on the pirate ship and its crew. None of the crew had seen him this mad and passionate about an enemy since he commanded the *Monitor*.

Again, the Dahlgrens barked their tunes of death. Flames brightened the fog bank and illuminated what had been the wheelhouse. This time, their fire obliterated the ship's wheelhouse and any remains of a former command center. The captain handed his spyglass to the lieutenant so he too could look upon the devastation that had once been a pirate ship. Remnants of what had been sails only minutes before were seen through the smoke and flames. A loud cheer went up across the deck, directed at the captain and his lieutenant. Each and every sailor on board was proud to serve under their leadership. Of course, this was no consolation to the remains of the pirate crew. The captain could have pulled alongside the pirate ship and brought the balance of the crew aboard, but it was the captain's decision, and his decision alone, to let them all go to Davy Jones' Locker during the next storm. Possibly, with a lot of luck, another ship would pass and save them. That was hardly likely, though.

Pirates were common in that part of the North Atlantic, especially the closer one came to North America. During the whole sea battle, the Scandinavians on board cowered in the coal holds. Unused to battle, they hid between cords of firewood and beneath anything that they could crawl under, including under women's dresses. Not knowing who or what was attacking their ship, they simply routed in every direction.

The smell of gunpowder filled the coal holds, along with a thick cloud of gun smoke. Children screamed throughout the whole sea battle, as they had never heard cannon fire before, much less an actual sea battle. Wives and mothers cried continuously and men all tried their hardest to look brave. What a joke! Each and every one of them trembled at what had transpired. Screaming could also be heard from the pirate ship out in the fog. The ship's sailors were pleading for someone to save them. They begged the captain to turn his ship and pick them up. But there was no response from the captain or any member of his crew. The captain felt their predicament was entirely the pirates' fault for thinking the ship they were attacking was just another defenseless passenger ship.

Snow was still falling; the main deck was solid white by now, which blended with the full white sails the crew had once again raised. The whiteness gave an eerie impression that they were on a ghost ship. As snow continued to fall, stairwells and ladders became increasingly slippery and anyone that ventured up on deck lost their balance and fell almost immediately. Many an immigrant came up on deck to relieve himself and was never seen again.

Eventually, the snow subsided, the wind increased, and the sails blossomed to their full magnificent glory.

As the sails filled and the ship's speed increased, thoughts of the pirates' attempt to take over the ship lessened. It would have been foolhardy for the captain to pick up the pirates still alive after the battle. The pirates, most likely, had numerous men severely wounded and the captain had no medical staff to care for them. His was by no means a hospital ship. No pirates could have ever imagined that this sleepy passenger ship was prepared to defend itself with ten Dahlgren cannons. Nor would they have known that her captain was the captain of the now famous ship, *Monitor.* Her captain, Lieutenant John Worden, a decorated war hero, was more experienced than any other on salt or fresh water. Indeed, he was certainly no one to pick a fight with and definitely not a battle. That evening, after hours of celebration and a wee bit too much rum, the captain staggered into the galley. There he found most of his crew. The captain poured himself another tall glass of rum from the bottle in his hip pocket. He looked at the crew and said, "Gather round, pull up a water barrel, and listen to my tale."

CHAPTER TWENTY-ONE

"Har, lads," said the captain. "Gather round and I'll tell ye the tale of buccaneers of the inland waters to where we're going. The lakes of Michigan, Superior, Ontario, and the like."

The captain was a fabulous storyteller normally, but when he drank his private rum, his stories were even better. More of the crew crowded into the galley, not wanting to miss any of the tale. The captain took a long swig of his precious rum and continued.

"Back afore when topsail schooners careened through the Great Lakes and keel boats floated like spring logjams down the northern rivers of North America, yes, lads, there were pirates on the inland waters too. Some were as fierce as Blackbeard and Jean Lafitte.

"Up 'ere on cold winter nights, they still spin tales of old James Jesse Strong. Old James, as he was called, ruled the inland waters like a king, while his corsairs plundered the local fishermen from islands called Hog, Squaw, and Whiskey. Then there's yarns 'bout the murderin' bushwhackers, Big and Little Harpe and Sam Mason, the soldier gone bad who became a river pirate and amassed tons of booty.

"'Ave ye heard bout the Booth monopoly, down in Chicago parts, and how the fishermen fought the Booths? Ain't no lumber hookers left to recall Chicago's timber pirates, who were losing their war with the American Navy and its great iron warship until they laid some gold on them politicians. The warship be the *Michigan,* but ye better leave the rest of the tale to da perfessers o' lernin."

The captain's speech had now become quite sluggish and slurred from his rum, but his mind was still sharp enough to continue his tale. He began again.

"The United States' iron warship, *Michigan,* be almost forgotten, as it ne'er fired a shot or fought a battle on the high seas or the inland waters. She was America's first iron warship. She were a paddle-wheel frigate launched to fight a war with Canada that never came to be. This was near twenty years afore John Ericsson's *Monitor.*

"Instead, the *Michigan* was used on the Great Lakes in her beginnings to enforce federal laws on the frontier waters of the lakes. In the first part of the last century, the Great Lakes were the main routes of Midwest trade. Even after the railroads came, the Great Lakes carried a good amount of freight. When commerce became successful, pirates were figuring different ways to partner into the trade without puttin' any money up front. The Barbary Coast of the rivers was the caves along the Ohio River in south Illinois. The pirates pillaged commerce shipping from 'ere."

Again the captain cleared his throat of dryness with another swig of rum. Tipping over slightly now, the captain said, "Lads, are ye still with me?" There was a collective, "Aye, Captain." The captain gave a signal for the lieutenant to move in closer and out of the doorway to hear the rest of the tale.

"If ye robbed a galleon or two, you got gold, but on the Great Lakes you wanted to rob a lumber ship or an ore boat." The captain spoke loudly now. "But no one would ever rob a passenger ship, especially a passenger ship with cannons. They surely won't get our ship, will they lads?"

"No sir, Captain," bellowed a crewmember, "not with our Dahlgrens."

The captain stumbled on with his tale, his eyes getting glassy. "Chicago's timber pirates operated on such a large scale that America's federal government sent the warship *Michigan* in to put the pirates out of business.

"The lumber barons down 'ere in Chicago and Milwaukee would poach timber from federal lands. Then they would ship the poached timber down to Chicago on lumber hookers, then send the timber west on the railroad. The federal government sent in a revenue agent, name of Isaac Willard. One night, the pirates came and burned down the inn that Willard was sleeping at. But Willard got out and stole a good amount of poached timber. Willard tried to sell it at auction in Chicago, but the pirates met him with a mob and ran him off. Willard was so mad that he called in the American navy. They sent in the *Michigan*. At first, the *Michigan* had been launched on the Great Lakes because the British were building warships left and right. Navy contractors had made a new ship that, when fitted out, would have new types of weapons, propulsion, and hull materials. She could outrun the fastest sailing frigate or destroy wooden warships with shells from pivoting guns on its centerline. The new warship was stronger, but lighter, and cheaper to build than the sturdiest wooden hulls."

"The *Michigan* and her eight-inch cannon chased lumber baron Ben Bagnall out of Chicago and up to Milwaukee, where he was arrested. The *Michigan* alone put timber pirates out of business. The lumber barons together with timber pirates went to the legislatures and had some laws changed. At the behest of the lumber industry, congress withdrew funding for the timber agencies that had been set up to enforce the federal poaching laws.

"With no agency and no money to enforce the law, timber piracy continued until the forests were exhausted. The *Michigan* then turned its attention north, up to the state of Michigan. Up in Michigan, there was a sect of Mormon privateers led by their leader, Beaver Island Strang. Strang had seized control of Beaver Island and was doing battle with local Irish gangs over fishing rights and boundaries. Strang was declared king of Beaver Island. These followers of Strang were referred to as 'Strangites.' They would steal off to harry the peaceful straits, pirating up and down bound traffic.

"Rock-strewn Indian Point was a favorite location for piracy of all types of shipping. The Strangites would light fires on shore to lure ships onto the rocks, then attack and loot the distressed ships. The ship's crews assumed the fires were channel lights and simply followed the lights in until crashing onto the rocks. This was piracy in a primitive form. The pirates assisted ships on the rocks. Once they assisted in any manner, the pirates automatically assumed they had the total rights to the contents. Under maritime law, if a ship was abandoned by its crew and captain, salvagers, or pirates, could legally take the ship and contents for their own. Whether they carried lumber, ore, Christmas trees, or passengers, all ships were helpless once lured onto Indian Point.

"The unwary passenger ships were a bonus to the pirates. Once the ship was locked onto the rocks, the passengers, mostly immigrants from Scandinavia, Germany, and Ireland, would gladly give up their worldly possessions, if only to be rescued and brought to shore in the pirates' longboats. It had become a full-fledged business. These pirates were heroes to some, but villains to all the rest.

"The Irish pirates, led by the four Martin brothers, were caught by the Mormons, beaten close to death, and then set adrift on a raft. The Martins were saved by some Indians in their canoes passing close to Garden Island several months later. The Martins had come over to the New World from Ireland, where all they knew was to steal for a profession. On Lake Michigan, the Beaver Island War between the Mormons and Irish ended, but not the piracy.

"When the *Michigan* pulled into St. James Harbor, its captain ordered Strang on board for a conference. Strang was assassinated by two of his men as he approached the *Michigan* for the conference and his body was thrown over-board. Strang had ordered his men to row their longboat over to the *Michigan.* He decided he would capitualate to the pressures put on him by the *Michigan's* intimidating presence. His men disagreed with cutting a deal. Soon after that, the Irish drove the Mormons from the island. The Irish gangs invited Mormon leaders to meet. When the Mormons drew close, the Irish opened fire, killing several and driving them off the island. To this day the Irish flag is flown on Beaver Island, along with the Stars and Stripes.

"Following these altercations, the *Michigan* was involved with a massive case of piracy on the Great Lakes. The Confederates called it 'privateering.' Whatever the terminology, it was sanctioned by the nations at war and named 'commerce raiding.'"

The captain had become very dry once again, although his speech had returned to normal.

"Lads, pass me over a stool," he said. "I am tiring down and my legs are getting old."

The captain continued with his tale. "It was soon after the Civil War began that Confederate officers in Richmond, Virginia, and their Confederate agents in British Canada began to plot ways to capture the *Michigan* and turn her eight-inch guns on Great Lakes cities, like Chicago.

"By 1863, the Confederate cause wasn't going any- where. The Confederates began to sink some serious money into attempts to disrupt the Union's industrial base. Confederate agents from Canada, pretending to be travelers, booked passage on the passenger steamer, *Phico-Parsons,* and seized her on Lake Erie. The Confederates followed by seizing the steamer, *Island Queen,* and headed for Sandusky, Ohio.

"In Sandusky, the *Michigan* was guarding a prisoner of war camp. The Canadian government got wind of the plot and seizure and contacted the United States Navy Department. The *Michigan* was warned and was ready.

"The Confederate agent that was supposed to poison the crew and give the signal to attack was arrested onboard the *Michigan* and the whole plot failed. The Confederate pirates steamed back to Canada with the *Michigan* in hot pursuit. The pirates escaped into Canada, taking with them both seized ships.

"The Irish fishermen on Beaver Island continued their plundering, and now took on Chicago's A. Booth and Sons. The Booths were the biggest threat to the Irish because they figured they were trying to monopolize the Great Lakes fishing industry.

"Alfred A. Booth came to Chicago from England and became a fish merchant. Booth's business was the biggest on the Great Lakes. Booth gathered forty-two other fish merchants in Chicago and formed a trust to control the fish- ing trade.

"In this time period most of the piracy on the Great Lakes consisted of local pirate gangs looting shipwrecks that had floundered onto the rocks or into shallow water caused by running into the rocks. These shipwrecks were

redundant

considered legal salvage after their crews abandoned the ships. The ships were quickly abandoned as the pirates arrived firing their weapons at the unarmed crewmembers. Once a ship was wrecked and the crew had abandoned it, the ship was then considered available for salvage."

The captain climbed down off his stool, staggered a bit, then stood up straight and said, "Lads, it is time to call it a night as I've finished my tale of the treacherous pirate scoundrels. I be hurried to hit the porcelain, too."

As the captain left the galley, one of the crew whispered to another, "Let's pilfer the pantry."

Another murmured, "Let's not."

CHAPTER TWENTY-TWO

The ship's passengers were awakened late one deathly cold and miserable night. There was screaming up on deck. Some thought the pirates had returned and others thought the ship was sinking. Neither was correct.

A somber quiet fell over the ship as everyone listened intently for something, anything. A loud cry came from the crow's nest. "Land ho!"

The crew had sighted landfall and it was dead ahead. The night was cold, clear, and crisp with a three-quarter moon. Every star was out that night. It was so clear you could see for ten miles. There was no mistaking the landmass dead in front of the ship. Following the crew's land sighting, wild laughter trumpeted across the deck. Loud English accents were the only voices heard up on deck. A passenger who could speak and understand English explained that the voices above were saying cruel and insulting things and were laughing at the immigrants down below deck.

The Holm family was by now at the stairwell in their coal hold. They listened to every word, even while not understanding a single one. Erick asked his mother, "Why are the crewmembers making fun of us?"

Mother simply said, "They simply don't understand us. Don't take it personally."

The captain gave approval to allow a few immigrants from each hold up to view the land sighting for themselves. The captain felt this sighting would entertain the immigrants' imaginations.

They were then told to promptly return below deck so that the business of operating the ship could return to normalcy. Indeed, the joke was truly on all those uneducated immigrants below deck in the coal holds. Most thought they were seeing their first view of America. That was not the case, as they would soon find out. The land sighting was not America but Halifax, Nova Scotia.

The ship continued north past Cape Breton Island and into the Cabot Strait. It continued across the Gulf of St. Lawrence and into the St. Lawrence River. Looking out over the ship's bow, as it slowly cut its way through the river, one could see Quebec, with Newfoundland to the north. Prince Edward Island and New Brunswick were to the south.

The captain steered his ship southwest toward Prince Edward Island. The island was a well-known location for restocking provisions after surviving the Devil's Doorway. The lighthouse at East Point on Prince Edward Island was where the Gulf of St. Lawrence meets the Northumberland Strait. This most famous reef was historically known to hide a whole group of shipwrecks. The reef became only a slim shadow at high tide.

Prince Edward Island is Canada's tiniest province, floating between New Brunswick and Nova Scotia. The island is only a spit of red dirt covered with potato farms. The ship moved closer and the crew witnessed the glaring red sand beaches along with the red cliffs that crumbled into the sea as the ship's waves brushed the soft red earth. A little fishing hamlet teetered precariously at the cliff's edges. Silence spread across the ship's deck as word passed that the captain would send in two longboats to the hamlet. The crewmembers would then travel by foot up to the hamlet. The ship's food stores needed replenishing and this seemed as good a location as any. The captain glassed the cliffs, settling on a lone white lighthouse and a church steeple capped by a spire. His spyglass was the forerunner of today's binoculars. With the lighthouse located where it was, it made the captain feel an immediate need to be on high alert for rocks. Even though the captain was a risk taker, this was not the time or place to meet his Waterloo.

One of the ship's crew assigned to the longboats was fluent in French. He would head the negotiations for all the needed provisions, as this was French Canadian territory. Topping the provision list was fresh fruit and vegetables. They knew getting such provisions would be highly unlikely. Next on the list were huge amounts of halibut and cod. The ship anchored in the St. Lawrence at eight fathoms, a safe five miles out in the river. The captain didn't want to become just another shipwreck on the treacherous reefs only to be found later in some old dusty historical records, with the caption, "Driven onto the reef by a buffoon as a captain." The ship was a safe distance from New Brunswick's mainland.

The ship spent the better part of a week anchored and transporting provisions from the sleepy little fishing hamlet back to the ship by longboats. The hamlet was home to French Canadian Voyageurs who wore plumes in their red hats and wide bright tight sashes to support their internal organs during grueling portages. The Voyageurs canoed over treacherous, turbulent, pounding rivers and waterfalls, ricocheting off immense boulders, their sash-type girdles saving them. They wore baggy white pantaloons, leather leggings, a loose blue chemise, and a red bandana. Without the Voyageurs' help, the provisions would have taken far longer to transport to the ship.

There were knife fights and drinking bouts, along with a sloppy feast on shore after the transporting of provisions was over. The Voyageurs cooked up a thick greasy duck soup and pemmican, unleavened bread along with eggs that still had the chickens in them for more protein. They cooked up cattails and served them like potatoes. For the first time in many weeks, a festive atmosphere took hold of the passengers and crew. The smell of burning oak once again came from the galley stoves.

Fresh fish was piled high in wooden crates, covered with ice chips and blocks. As fast as the longboats could transport the crates to the ship, the passengers would help haul the heavy crates up the side of the ship using come-alongs, then block and tackle to lift them up over the sides and to the cleaning tables temporarily set up on deck. Scaling, gutting, quartering, and cleaning were followed by moving the fish to the galley stoves. There, an assembly line of cooks would fry and boil up the hundreds of cod and halibut.

With their stores replenished, the ship was on the move again. As they came along the river, they could see some of the oldest rock formations known to science. These were the rocks of the original North American continent, and they got there from volcanic events that had happened 2.7 billion years before. The formations had also been helped along by glaciers that had gouged out this panoramic scene that Erick was witnessing. They continued following the St. Lawrence River past the Gaspe Peninsula.

For the first time in a month, you could hear the crew chanting sailing songs as they went about their individual duties. The ship was on course, the exact course that the captain had originally intended to take. They were heading

where most ship's captains carrying illegal immigrants steered their ships and that was through America's Backdoor. The St. Lawrence River was used as the main route of the undocumented, unauthorized immigrants coming into America.

As the ship proceeded down along the St. Lawrence, land could be seen on each side of the ship. The last storm the ship had gone through turned out to be quite normal whenever a ship passed the coastal waters of Nova Scotia. Seasoned sailors knew this area of the North Atlantic Ocean as the Devil's Doorway, which correctly described the last three hundred miles. Those frightening, howling winds that cut across the ship, from bow to stern were known as the Devil's Symphony. As the ship passed between these two massive parcels, everything seemed more peaceful and tranquil. Being forty miles across, it didn't seem at all like a river. Instead of being on a river, the passengers felt they were sailing on one of the great lakes of Sweden.

Looking southward down the St. Lawrence, the great river didn't seem to be going anywhere in particular. For thousands of years before the white man ever came to North America, the St. Lawrence River was an Indian highway known as "The River With No End." Jacques Cartier was the first explorer known to have visited the St. Lawrence. His ships were forced to stop at Montreal, Canada because of the Lachine Rapids. These rapids remained an obstacle for all but a few daredevils who would shoot the rapids. The British are credited for building the first locks around the rapids.

Music could be heard coming from down in the coal holds. The mood of the immigrants had turned from somber to outright gaiety since reaching the St. Lawrence. Erick frolicked with little Charles on the lower steps of the hold. The two of them would dart back and forth between the cavernous holds where the precious coal was piled high like mountains. The coal laid and waited for the call to be hustled into the furnaces.

A sense of survival, stirred together with ample amounts of happiness, had taken hold of the immigrants. Most of the immigrants had survived the voyage. So very many had died along the way and would never enjoy the benefits of the New World, but those that did survive were now hopeful of finding a better life in America. The word "homesteader" had been on the lips of the immigrants since sailing from Göteborg. Erick's Grandfather Ernst had spoken the American word quite frequently. A homesteader was an individual that was granted 160 acres of public land for $1.25 an acre. The land had to be improved within five years, plus lived on for six months. It was free until all the requirements were satisfied. The Swedish understanding that children should be seen and not heard always prevented Erick from interrupting at family discussions to ask what this word meant.

Stories from returning seamen coming back from America told that the better life had been discovered in America. There were the gold rushes at Frazer Valley, British Columbia, and Sutter's Mill in California. It was expensive for Swedish men to bring their families to North America. Because of this, many of the first immigrant communities were predominantly bachelor societies. Most lived with loneliness, hardship, hard work, alienation, and the discriminatory taunts about being dumb Swedes. The married men would pinch every penny to bring their wives and children to North America. They had learned to become exceptionally thrifty in saving for their families.

Anna Holm had a difficult time adjusting to her new life, new language, new land, and new values. Family conflicts escalated into overwhelming life changes. She found there was no easy escape from the tragic past and that her family's history did not release itself easily. Anna was haunted by her family's dismal existence in Sweden, her soul-searching as to whether their life could repeat itself in America, their miraculous survival on the coffin ship while so many parished, and the possible futility of her struggle.

Farmers and their families almost immediately began packing their picks, shovels, and hoes for the better life. They left their communal, sharecropping farms in exchange for the American government's offer of free homesteader land.

They sailed on past Quebec City and Montreal. The ship reached the first of the Great Lakes, Lake Ontario, and the end of salt water.

Approaching Hamilton, Ontario, the sails came down and the engine was powered once again by steam. The precious coal was finally shoveled into the furnaces and the big furnaces fired right up. Passengers were pleasantly overwhelmed with long forgotten happy feelings. Joy and warmth overcame them, as did the furnace heat. This surprise of the furnaces being turned on was an immediate feeling of heat in the belly of the beast. Whole families wept from the pleasure of it. The warm heat was subtle at first, but then it slowly cascaded from hold to hold. It was as if they had been transported in front of a roaring fireplace hearth back in Sweden. Heat that the passengers had longed for quickly turned into intense, suffocating, and stifling heat. The heat in the holds had come up so fast and had become so hot that all the ship's rats ran out of their holes. The rats ran up and over the families of immigrants in a desperate effort to escape. Screaming women and children ran in all directions, dressed only in their frumpish underthings. The ship had been full of rats throughout the voyage, but they never came out all at once before.

The men were trying as best as they could to club them to death with hoes, shovels, and rakes. It soon became a hopeless endeavor. Everyone finally gave up emotionally to the now-clear fact that the rats were passengers too.

The heat radiated from the coal-fired furnaces in the compartment next to Erick's bed of straw, the same compartment where Erick and little Charles had played hide-and-seek for over six weeks. If they could have walked on water to reach America, they certainly would have tried.

Again the immigrants were surprised as the furnaces were shut down as suddenly as they had been turned on. Erick and the family dragged out their warm clothing and blankets again. At the same time, Erick noticed that the rats were running back into their holes. As everyone got used to the cold again, the sails came down abruptly and the furnaces fired right back up, replacing sails through another treacherous body of water, until reaching Lake Huron, the third American Great Lake.

The ship plowed effortlessly through Lake Huron and past Mackinaw City, Michigan, with its furnaces fired up to full capacity. Mackinaw City was known as one of the coldest locations in all of North America. The captain had the sails hoisted and they exploded into a full billowing white bloom. It seemed like the ship had taken on a life of its own as it sped across Lake Huron. It was so cold here that the crew even asked the captain to turn on the furnaces. The weather had once again turned fierce and had developed into a full-blown ice storm. Ice rapidly covered the bow, deck, and helmsmen house. Ice covered the manropes and even went down to the deck planks. The captain was forced to lower the sails for fear of damaging them. They forged on into Lake Michigan, the fourth Great Lake, and south down the long lake directly into the storm. They passed Escanaba, Michigan, and Menominee and Manitowac, Wisconsin.

The captain had a message passed on to the passengers. The message was that the first debarkation point would be coming up within hours. Those that wanted to get off were free to do so, even if they had originally signed up to go further. The first debarkation point would not be Delaware, New Jersey, or New York, but Milwaukee, Wisconsin. There was no Coast Guard, radar, or sonar to detect these illegals.

Dropping off illegals in the 1880s actually proved quite simple. It was easy to get all the way to Milwaukee without being detected. Maneuvering a ship through America's Backdoor was easy. Ellis Island didn't officially open until 1892. Until that time, America was like a sieve and the immigrants poured through like water from a faucet. The ship anchored off Milwaukee as hundreds of passengers disembarked one by one and were transported by longboats. The others left on board wanted to go on to the last debarkation point, which was Chicago, Illinois.

That night, the ship stayed at Milwaukee so the crew could rest up after transporting so many souls, belongings, and animals to shore by longboat. The following morning the furnaces had to be turned on due to the lack of wind. It was a short trip of about ninety miles, which to these immigrants took forever. They were heading south to the largest American industrial port at the time. The industrial city of Chicago came into sight and word was passed down to the coal holds. The majority of passengers that were still on board were Swedish. The dream of the Holm family was about to come true.

The ship anchored approximately three miles out in Lake Michigan. It anchored off of Foster Avenue on the north side of Chicago, known as "Swede Town." South of Foster Avenue was Chicago Avenue, which was called the

"Swedish Snoose Boulevard." Anchoring three miles out was necessary, first, because the ship was carrying illegals and second, because Lake Michigan was too shallow, even far out offshore. The lakeshore at Foster Avenue was one long pristine sand beach and was in fact so shallow that it could have been a giant wading pool. One could walk out a thousand yards and still not be completely covered by water. In fact, the ship anchored where Chicago's beautiful Outer Drive is today.

The Swedes left the ship on longboats. The crew would row them in until they became stuck in the sand. Once they were stuck, over the sides the immigrants had to go, into the freezing Lake Michigan water up to their hips. They were unable to row in any further due to the shallowness.

From the time of boarding in Göteborg, Sweden, until stepping foot on America's soil took the Holm family sixteen weeks. The finest ships of that day (and the ship they had been on was certainly not one of them) only took six to ten weeks to reach Delaware.

Unable to find lodging the first night in America, a kindly Swedish family took the Holm family into their home that night. The community at Foster Avenue was, as it turned out, Chicago's Swedish community. This was no accident. The captain had been dropping off his illegal Swedish immigrants for years, right at this same location. At the time, Chicago Swedes occupied the area from Lake Michigan to west past Clark Street, which is now known as Andersonville. At that time, Clark Street was only a muddy road of wagon ruts that had originally been an Indian trail. Chicago was not a genteel nineteenth-century city, but a lurid assemblage of rowdies and hoodlums along the lakefront. It was a veritable ghetto of saloons and bordellos, with their harlots. Gambling halls and rampant corruption were the sinful side of the city. Large farms of cabbages and potatoes covered the area as far as the eye could see. The Europeans did the bulk of the farming. They also bought up the prairies and sand flats. These immigrants from Ireland, Germany, England, and Luxembourg bought everything in sight. The largest purchase of land was accomplished by Philip McGregor Rogers of County Louth, Ireland. This flat land was originally the encampment of the last of the Native Americans, which were forced out in 1830.

The Holm family finally settled in Andersonville at 1929 Berwyn Avenue.

No brief survey could possibly do justice to the scope and variety of achievements of the first Swedish element in Chicago. Most of the immigrants were farmers and the total area they first put under their plows was comparable to that cultivated at the time by all their kinsmen in Sweden. Thousands of others became loggers, miners, or railroad construction workers. Large numbers took construction jobs in Chicago. In fact, Swedish immigrants built large parcels of Chicago's earliest buildings. In early Chicago, Swedish immigrants made substantial contributions as workers, foremen, engineers, inventors, managers, and risk-taking leaders.

AFTERWORD

The Holm family's safe arrival in America began a new dimension in their lives. Erick immediately made friends with children his own age in the neighborhoods of Andersonville. He found that all of the children were originally from Sweden. They would compare stories and play together in play lots. Erick and little Charles passed their time playing stickball, the rage of Chicago at the time. Johan Holm was offered employment the day after arriving in Chicago, as a mill hand at a nearby foundry.

The Holm family stayed a month with the kindly Swedish family that took them in the first night. Some time after, they rented a flat and settled into America comfortably. Johan and Anna immediately sent letters of invitation off to their parents and grandparents in Sweden, urging them to immigrate to Chicago. One year later, Grandfather Ernst and Grandmother Anna walked down a gang plank in Chicago. Tears of happiness were shed by all and smiles radiated between them.

The years passed quickly. Erick fished along Chicago's Lake Michigan shores and hunted pheasants and rabbits with his newly-received Christmas rifle. He worked at his uncle's potato farm in Lincolnwood, Illinois during the summer.

What about honesty.

The Holm family was under pressure to create their own identity. They wanted to break out of the Swedish mold, learn American skills and the English language. Erick and little Charles learned the language quickly at Trumbell School on Foster Avenue. Johan and Anna added to their family with the addition of David Ernst and Esther. There were many children from Andersonville coming over to play and visit with the boys and now, the baby girl. The chidren would always say "Let's go over to the Holmes." Johan and Anna heard the saying "Holmes" so often that they eventually changed their name from Holm to Holmes.

Little Charles couldn't stop growing and ended up being six-feet, six-inches tall. After graduating from Central High School, Erick found himself a steady girl named Meta Seydel. In 1901, Erick and Meta were married. His best man was, of course, Little Charles and the maid of honor was Esther. Erick and his bride, nicknamed Mattie, started a family, beginning with a set of twins, Oliver and Mabel, who were quickly followed by another boy, Alfred. By now, Erick had become a tailor and opened his own little store front.

David, Erick's brother, began courting a woman named Vera Mae. Little Charles never married, and David and he bought a couple of trucks and started hauling bricks. Not long after that, David and Vera married and had three sons—Floyd, Calvin, and David Alfred. By now, everyone had changed their name to Holmes. Erick's family wasn't complete until Raymond, Dorothy, Gladys, Donald, and Eleanor were born.

Erick made quite a name for himself in tailoring and attracted many of Chicago's well-to-do. One such customer was Daniel Burnham, the architect and philanthropist. Erick and Burnham struck up a friendship and bonded like brothers. Burnham thought Erick could do much better for himself and his family. He made contact with the mayor of Chicago and Erick was quickly hired. He started as Assistant to the Park District Director in 1908 at the age of thirty. Erick was in a position now to show his talent and his ability to toot his own horn. One might say that Erick fell into a perfect world with Burnham. It was, however, short-lived, because in 1912 Burnham died. Considering Erick's close association with Burnham, all could have ended with his death. However, Erick had become his own man and his work was massive and endless due to the Chicago fire.

One day Dorothy, Erick's fifteen-year-old daughter, answered the phone. This call was to notify the Holmes family that Erick, their father and husband, had suffered a massive heart attack at his desk and died at the age of 47. In those days, wakes were held in the parlor of the family home. One by one, the mourners filed through the back door into the parlor and out the front door. There were almost a thousand visitors, including the mayor of Chicago. This was 1925. Several of Erick's children were young and were forever burdened through their lives by their father's untimely death. Raymond, Dorothy, and Gladys had to quit high school to help their mother make ends meet and keep the family home. Oliver and Raymond started a trucking company, O&R Trucking.

Erick, Meta, his wife, and their children, Alfred, Oliver, Dorothy, Gladys, and Eleanor are all interned in the family plot at Rosehill Cemetery in Chicago, Illinois. Erick's father Johan, his mother, Anna, and their children Little Charles and Esther are interned along with David and his wife Vera Mae at Memorial Cemetery, Skokie, Illinois.

So ends America's Backdoor.

Holmes Family Tree

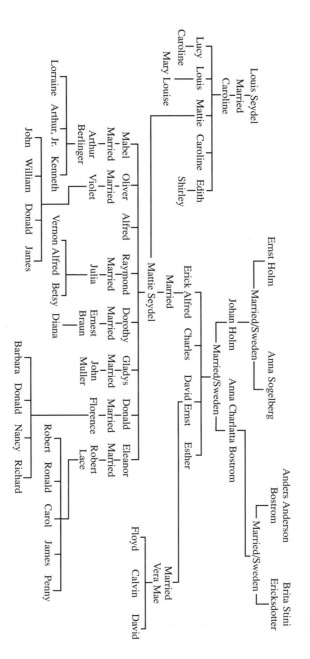

Hand-carved model of the ship
that transported Erick to America.

Meta "Mattie" Seydel Holmes
Wife of Erick Holmes

Six of Erick Holmes' eight children
Left to right:
Front: Eleanor, Donald, Raymond
Rear: Mabel, Dorothy, Gladys

The Holmes Family *Left to right:*
Front: Oliver, Erick, Johan, Alfred, Raymond, Anna, Meta, Baby Dorothy
Rear: Esther, Little Charles, Vera Mae, David Ernst, Mabel

HISTORICAL NOTES

The ship, *Sleipner,* was the first schooner to brave the high seas coming directly from mainland Europe. If, in fact, the *Sleipner* had not cut its trail through the Great Lakes, the Holms would never have settled in Chicago. They most likely would have settled on the east coast of America. She came down through the Great Lakes to Chicago and was the original trailblazer to do so. Her captain, Vaage, manned the schooner on four consigned trips from Bergen, Norway, to Chicago. Cargo that was obtained in the Civil War filled the schooner on return trips. On August 2, 1862, the *Sleipner* arrived with 107 passengers and 350 tons of cargo. The *Sleipner* was met on each trip with full gun salutes, City of Chicago officials, and Captain Jennings' marching band. The band members were all of Scandinavian descent and volunteered their time to play when passenger ships from their homeland were scheduled to arrive. The local Nora Lodge and Norwegian residents met the weary travelers of the seventy-one day trip. The Nora Lodge was a Norwegian volunteer society. They hosted funerals and weddings at no expense to the families. It was similar to today's "welcome wagon."

The Civil War and the Sioux Indian outbreak were great hardships to the immigrants going into Minnesota, Iowa, the

Dakotas, and Wisconsin. In 1863, the small schooner, *Skjoldmoen,* arrived in Chicago with six men and a dog from Norway. The next small schooner was the *Arendal.* Only a few of the immigrants that arrived in 1862 remained at Kinzie Street. It has been estimated that 6,000 people have descended from those first 107 *Sleipner* passengers. The *Sleipner* paved the way for overseas immigrants to arrive in America via the Great Lakes.

The earliest organized endeavor to promote the best interests of seamen on the Chicago waterfront appears to have been the founding on July 10, 1842, of the Mariners Temperance Society. Its leaders provided improvised services for seamen on the wharves of the harbor. These efforts were reinforced by the founding on December 19, 1843, of a Chicago Bethel Association, committed to promoting the gospel on ship and shore. The following year, a Seamen's Bethel Church was built on Wells Street. This simple wooden chapel was run by the Seamen's Friend Society, a society involved with ministry to seafarers in both Britain and America.

Chicago Bethel soon became the center of a thriving maritime ministry, at once both international and interdenominational. As the number of Scandinavian lake seamen increased, the chapel became too small to minister to them. In 1869, the twenty-five-year-old Seamen's Bethel was replaced by a larger church built of brick on Michigan Avenue and Market Street. It was comprised of a sanctuary, but also a reading room and library.

By the turn of the century, steamers had largely superseded the old lake schooners. Many Swedes joined the Lake Michigan steamer fleet. Then came the advent of diesel power along with ship owners developing shallow-draft, narrow-beam, and oceangoing motor vessels specially designed for linking the Great Lakes port of Chicago with

Europe. In the meantime, Chicago churches, as well as other organizations, made a practice of contacting seafaring countrymen calling on Chicago.

The Salvation Army, with Colonel Tom Gabrielsen at the helm, deserves much of the credit for ministering to Chicago's seamen. Chicago, linking Lake Michigan with the Gulf of Mexico via the Mississippi River, rapidly became the world's greatest inland port. However, after the completion of the Welland Canal in 1833, Chicago also obtained access to the Atlantic Ocean via the St. Lawrence River System.

In the development of Chicago as a major overseas port, Swedes again played a pioneering role. A plaque at the northwest corner of the State Street Bridge over the Chicago River marks the mooring place of the Norwegian Brig, *Sleipner,* as the first vessel direct from Europe, destined for Chicago. The *Sleipner* arrived from Bergen, Norway, August 2, 1862, and was loaded, according to the *Chicago Tribune* of the day, with sturdy Norwegian farmers and their bouncing wives and children.

Chicago was home to thousands of schooners in 1886. Chicago's port was busier than the ports of New York, New Orleans, Boston, and San Francisco combined. With the shipping industry increasingly turning to furnace-powered steamers, they could handle larger passenger and industrial loads.

Schooner captains had to find new niches for profit, so they shifted to high-profit cargo, transporting iron ore, coal, wheat, corn, and Christmas trees. The captains knew it was a risky proposition, because insurers would refuse to cover them when loading to full capacity. In addition, insurers feared winter storms would create additional wrecks. Still, captains were unwilling to brave winter's worst or risk sailing their finest ships into harm's way. In many documented cases, the shipping industry often made their winter voyages using second-rate ships that should have been in dry dock and were well past their prime for safe sailing. It was a foregone conclusion that the schooners would cross the Great Lakes virtually sheathed in ice. Every captain was aware of the extreme dangers of sailing on the Great Lakes in November or December. A sure sign of imminent danger would be the fact that the rats would leave the ships at port. Captains noticing the departing rats would normally refuse to sail any further than the rats. It usually proved to be an accurate indication of safety. Sheathed ice would weigh the ship down and the crews would have to chop the ice loose at each port. Many questionably seaworthy schooners were recaulked in hopes they could make yet another risky voyage beyond the limits of safe shipping.

In the winter, one major industry in Chicago was ice. Before the days of electric refrigeration, the only means of keeping food and potables from perishing was to put them on ice. Frozen blocks of ice were harvested from nearby lakes, then packed and shipped to Chicago. Farming the ice took gangs of several hundred Scandinavians. They were brought out to the Chain of Lakes in Lake County. The Chicago meat packers required fresh ice for their meat. They built massive ice houses along the lakes, sixty miles north of Chicago. The Swedish ice cutters stayed in attached rooming houses. Swedes with horse-drawn saws trekked onto the lake's frozen surface out in temperatures that dipped to twenty below zero. They would cut ice blocks that were slightly smaller than bales of hay. The gigantic cubes were hauled to shore by horse or sometimes floated through manmade channels for their trip to the icehouses.

Immigrants were no strangers to hard, heavy, back-breaking work. They often worked in cavernous buildings where ice blocks were packed tightly in hay to keep them frozen. Most icehouses had adjoining lodgings for the seasonal Scandinavian workers who stayed during the ice harvest. Chicago's meatpacking plants were the largest consumers of ice blocks. Large meatpacking firms like Armour and Nel's Morris invested heavily in the production of ice during the winter. All ice was shipped by rail to Chicago.

These uneducated Swedes worked hard and were called "dumb Swedes" due to the fact that no one else would touch the degrading and humiliating work that the Swedes accepted readily and willingly. They commonly worked on projects like digging latrines, shoveling garbage, cleaning fish, ice farming, septic cleaning and the seasonal picking of vegetables.

In 1900, Chicago had 1,700,000 inhabitants, of which the Swedish-born numbered 49,000. This figure was exceeded by only three cities in Sweden. If the 49,000 Swedish immigrants were included, Chicago would have ranked as the second largest Swedish city in the world after Stockholm, Sweden's capitol.

Minnesota received more immigrants from Sweden than any other state in the U.S. The census of 1910 reported about 122,000 Swedish-born citizens. Illinois came next with 115,000. Today, about half of Sweden's inhabitants have relatives in America. Not that far from Chicago, many Swedes also started a Swedish colony. In Pepin County, Wisconsin on the Mississippi River is Lake Pepin, home to Wisconsin's "Little Sweden," which is Stockholm, Wisconsin. The first Swedish log home in the county was built in 1856 on Lake Pepin. In 1867, Laura Ingalls Wilder was born in a log home seven miles northwest of Pepin. Her first book, written when she was sixty-five, was *Little House in the Big Woods*. Her family immigrated from Sweden.

Erickson Point in the village of Stockholm offers the most scenic view of the river. The Swedish heritage of Stockholm has continued to be very important even today. In the early 1640s, colonists bought land from the Indians as far west as the sunset and their territory finally comprised nearly all of present-day Delaware, eastern Pennsylvania, and parts of Maryland and New Jersey. Most of the land for Philadelphia, including the site of Independence Hall, was purchased for William Penn from Swedish farmers. Sweden's government sent ministers for the religious and educational needs of the settlers. New churches were built and five such "Old Swedes," as the churches on the Delaware River are called, are still in use. Holy Trinity in Wilmington, Delaware was completed in 1699, and is the oldest church in the United States, standing as originally built and is still used for regular worship. Holy Trinity is now a national shrine. Due to the contributions of its natives, the heritage of Scandinavia will never be forgotten.

Famous Swedes

In navigation: John Ericsson invented the screw for navigation. He also designed a new type of gunboat, the first of which was named the *Monitor,* and gave the Civil War Union forces maritime supremacy.

In literature: The greatest author of Swedish ancestry is Carl Sandberg.

In medicine: The American father of surgery is Anton Carlson.

In nuclear research: Carl Anderson and Glen Seaborg were Nobel Prize winners.

Early painters include Adolph Wertmuller, who painted several portraits of George Washington, one of which hangs in the White House today.

Jenny Lind, the Swedish nightingale, will always hold a prominent place in the history of American song.

The Swedish share in American film circles includes Greta Garbo and Ingrid Bergman who studied at the Royal Dramatic Theater in Stockholm.

The most famous Swedish meteorologist was Carl Gustaf Rossby. Dr. Rossby successfully picked the invasion date for the Normandy invasion of World War II. As chairman of the meteorology department at the University of Chicago, he discovered the "Rossby Wave," a large symmetrical undulation that develops in a jet stream's axis of flow and separates cold polar air from warm tropical air. He also designed mathematical models for weather prediction. Other great names in aviation include Charles Lindbergh and Eric Nelson, who piloted the first Army air trip around the world. Also known for aviation technology is Philip Johnson, head of Boeing Aircraft.

In the automotive industry, contributions were made by Vincent Bendix, as well as Carl Edward Johansson, who was an associate of Henry Ford.

In ordnance, there was no one more important than John Adolph Dahlgren and his cannons which, in conjunction with John Ericsson's revolving turret revolutionized ordnance on ships and land.

Ellis Island

Ellis Island opened on January 1, 1892. The main building was wooden with a blue slate roof. Five years later, in a fire of mysterious origin, the main building and most of the other buildings on Ellis Island burned to the ground. Amazingly, no one was killed, but immigration records dating back to 1855 were destroyed. For the next five years, immigration offices were moved to the barge office in lower Manhattan.

Most immigrants were dirt poor. They came to the United States in the steerage sections of ships. This is the area directly below sea level, where the steering mechanism is located. Steerage was crowded, dark, and damp. There was no fresh air or fresh water. Sanitary conditions were not adequate. Out-breaks of contagious diseases were common. What little food the steamship company provided was often covered with maggots. In good weather, steerage passengers were sometimes permitted on deck for fresh air and exercise.

Angel Island in San Francisco Bay was one of the entry points into America. This entry was primarily for Asian immigrants. The main position of inspectors there, however, was to exclude Chinese aliens who were denied entry by the Chinese Exclusion Act of 1882. Anti-Asian prejudice sprang from racism and the the fact that Asian laborers competed with native workers for jobs. There were other entry points, such as Boston, Providence, Baltimore, and Philadelphia. Ellis Island's entry point into America had opened in 1892 with United States' government restrictions. The government had specific ideas about who was not welcome to stay. The Immigration Act of 1891 excluded mentally disabled individuals, those with a "loathsome or contagious disease," anyone that had been convicted of a crime, and those who might become financially dependent on the government.

Long before the island was named Ellis Island, Native Americans called it Kilshk, or Gull Island. There they would dig for clams and oysters. In the 1770s, Samuel Ellis, a merchant and fisherman, bought the island. Later, the federal government assumed control of it and stored ammunition there. On occasion pirates would be executed on the island. In 1890, President Benjamin Harrison ordered the ammunition removed so an immigration center could be built. The Statue of Liberty was a gift to the United States from the people of France. The statue was erected on Bedloe's Island, about 1,700 feet south of Ellis Island. A proposal to locate the immigration center on Bedloe's Island was defeated by those who did not want poor immigrants so close to a national shrine.

Steerage passengers were brought to Ellis Island in ferry boats, where they proceeded to the main building. About 5,000 immigrants could be processed each day. First- and second-class passengers, who paid more for their steamship tickets than steerage passengers, didn't have to go to Ellis Island. Inspectors came aboard ship to process them. With the large crowds, the many languages being spoken, and the general confusion, it was not surprising that some immigrants left Ellis Island with new names. In fact, some names may have been changed on the ship's list of passengers, before immigrants ever got to Ellis Island.

Inspectors began evaluating immigrants as they were moving from ship to shore. Immigrants could leave their baggage in baggage rooms. From the baggage rooms, immigrants went up a staircase. They did not know it, but inspection had already begun from the top of the stairs. Doctors watched for lameness or shortness of breath. If an inspector decided that further examination was needed in a particular area, an immigrant's coat would be marked with chalk. Chalk marks on clothing showed health problems and an X showed suspected mental defect. An X with a circle around it meant definite mental disease. Back problems were represented by a capital B. A capital C meant conjunctivitis. A capital E meant a problem with eyes. A chalk mark with an FT indicated a foot problem. A capital G meant a goiter. Suspected heart problems were identified by an H. A capital K meant a hernia. A capital L represented lameness. A capital N indicated a neck problem. A capital P meant a physical and lung problem. Pregnancies were marked as PG. A capital SC meant an obvious scalp problem. And finally, a capital S indicated senility.

Over the years, Ellis Island grew with the addition of landfills. Much of the fill came from the ships' balast (material carried in the holds of the ships to give them stability). Island #2 was created in 1899 and became the site of several hospital buildings. The hospital for contagious diseases was located on Island #3, built up in 1906. Eventually the space between the two hospital islands was filled in to become one.

A 1903 law kept out anarchists, and a 1917 law banned those who could not read in their own language or English. Ellis Island inspectors had to weed out the immigrants who fell into these categories. Still, only two percent were turned away. Inspectors registered the names of those who passed the legal test and gave them "landing cards." Sick immigrants were treated in various island hospital buildings. Sadly, over 3,500 immigrants died on Ellis Island.

About twenty out of every one hundred were detained for further inspection. For the detainees, the island became an island of tears. Detainees were kept in roms called pens. These dirty, wire-enclosed cells were designed to hold about six hundred people but, at times, up to 1,700 detainees were packed into one pen. About 2,000 immigrants per night were housed in overcrowded, pest-ridden dormitory rooms. They slept on wire mesh or canvas beds with no mattresses. Each immigrant was issued two blankets, which were often infested with lice, despite the fact that the people being held were deloused and their clothes were disinfected. Detainees who were eventually allowed to leave Ellis Island were often met by relatives at the Kissing Post, an area where family and friends embraced detainees who had received permission to leave.

SOURCES

The following books and tape were sources for research that appear and are recommended for those readers interested in pursuing further their study of this period of history.

Arnold, Barton H., *A Folk Divided: Homeland Swedes and Swedish Americans.* Southern Illinois University Press, 1994.

Bears, Edwin C., *Hardluck Ironclad.* Louisiana State University Press, 1966.

Buel, C. C., and Robert U. Johnson, *Battles and Leaders of the Civil War.* Castle Books.

Catton, Bruce, *The Civil War.* Bonanza Books distributed by Crown Publishing, Inc.

Catton, Bruce, *The Civil War.* Viking/Penguin Group, 1996.

Catton, Bruce, *Never Call Retreat.* New York: Doubleday & Company, 1965.

Catton, Bruce, *Terrible Swift Sword.* New York, Doubleday & Company, 1963.

Catton, Bruce, *Two Roads to Sumter.* New York, Doubleday & Company, 1960.

Cochran, Hamilton, *Blockade Runners of the Confederacy.* Bobbs-Merrill, 1958.

Cozzens, Peter, *No Better Place to Die.* University of Illinois, 1990.

Davis, William C., *Duel Between the First Ironclads.* Louisiana State University, 1975.

Hoglund, William A., *Finnish Immigrants in America.* University of Wisconsin Press, 1960.

Jones, Prof. Gwyn, *Atlantic Saga.* Oxford University Press.

Jones, Virgil Carrington, *The Civil War at Sea,* (3 volumes). Holt, Rinehart and Winston, 1960.

Jordan, Terry and Matti Kaups Jordan, *The American Backwoods Frontier.* Johns Hopkins University Press, 1989.

Ljungmark, Lars, *Swedish Exodus.* Southern Illinois University Press, 1973.

Milligan, John D., *Gunboats Down the Mississippi.* Annapolis: Naval Institute Press, 1965.

Murphy, Jim, *Gone A-Whaling.* New York: Clarion Books, a Houghton Mifflin Company, 1998.

Nelson, Helge, *The Swedes and the Swedish Settlements in North America.* Skrifter Utgivna av Kungl, Humanistiska vetenskapssamfundt i Lund Sweden, 1943.

Reimers, David M., *Ethnic Americans: A History of Immigration.* Columbia University Press.

Reimers, David M., *Unwelcome Strangers: American Identity and the Turn Against Immigration.* Columbia University Press.

Swanberg, W. A., *The Story of Fort Sumter: First Blood.* New York: Charles Scribner and Sons, 1957.

Tryckare, Tre, *The Viking.* Italy: Crown Publishing, Inc., 1972.

From Sweden to America: A History of the Migration. Edited by Harald Runblom and Hans Norman. University of Minnesota Press, 1976.

Migration from Finland to North America Between 1862 and the First World War by Institute of Migration Studies, CI, 1974.

Britannica World Language Dictionary. Funk and Wagnalls Company, 1956.

Compton's Encyclopedia and Fact-Index. 1990.

The New Encyclopaedia Britannica, 1988.

The Oxford Dictionary of Quotations. Oxford University Press, 1955.

The World Book Encyclopedia, 2001.

"Ellis Island," *Kids Discover Magazine.* May 2002.

Scandinavian Roots-American Lives by Nordic Council of Ministers, Berlings Skogs AB, Trelleborg, Sweden, 2000.

Swedish American Genealogist. Publisher: Swenson Swedish Immigration Research Center, June 1998.

Swedish American Genealogist. Publisher: Swenson Swedish Immigration Research Center. December 1999.

The principal periodicals on Nordic immigration and Nordic American history are: *Norwegian-American Studies,* published since 1926 by the Norwegian-American Historical Association; *The Swedish-American Historical Quarterly,* published since 1950 by the Swedish-American Historical Society; *The Bridge,* published since 1977 by the Danish-American Heritage Society; *The Bridge,* published by the Emigrant Register in Karlstad, Sweden; and the *Swedish-American Genealogist,* since 1980, published by Swenson Swedish Immigration Research Center.

American Cetacean Society, P.O. Box 2639, San Pedro, CA 90731.

American Swedish Institute, 2600 Park Ave., Minneapolis, MN 55407.

Cetacean Research Unit, P.O. Box 159, Gloucester, MA 01930.

Cetacean Society International, P.O. Box 9145, Wethersfield, CT 06109.

Cousteau Society, 930 West 21st Street, Norfolk, VA 23517.

Federation of Swedish Genealogical Societies: Hakan Skogsjo Tordmulegrand 6 FINN-22100 Mariehamn, Finland.

The Finnish-American Heritage Center, 601 Quincy, Hancock, Michigan 49930.

Greenpeace USA, 1436 U Street, NW, Washington, DC 20009.

Swedish-American Center of Chicago, 5211 N. Clark Street, Chicago, IL 60640.

Swedish-American Historical Society, North Park University, 5125 N. Spaulding Ave., Chicago, IL 60625.

The Swedish Emigrant Institute, P.O. Box 201 S-351 04, Vaxjo, Sweden.

Swedish-Finn Historical Society, P.O. Box 17264, Seattle, WA 98107.

Swedish Historical Society, 404 S. Third Street, Rockford, IL 61104.

Swenson Swedish Immigration Research Center, Augustana College, 639-38th Street, Rock Island, IL 61202.

WGBH Educational Foundation, Public Television.

Bergen Maritime Museum, Bergen, Norway.

Gothenburg Maritime Museum, Gothenburg, Sweden.

Gothenburg University Library, Gothenburg, Sweden.

Royal Library of Sweden, Stockholm, Sweden.

Swedish State Historical Museum, Stockholm, Sweden.

Lincoln's Secret Weapon, a NOVA Production by Zoe TV.